An Cosaert
Securing Your Business

An Cosaert

Securing Your Business

A practical guide to IP strategy and business growth

DE GRUYTER

ISBN 978-3-11-167306-6
e-ISBN (PDF) 978-3-11-167354-7
e-ISBN (EPUB) 978-3-11-167437-7

Library of Congress Control Number: 2025940068

Bibliographic information published by the Deutsche Nationalbibliothek
The Deutsche Nationalbibliothek lists this publication in the Deutsche Nationalbibliografie;
detailed bibliographic data are available on the Internet at http://dnb.dnb.de.

© 2026 Walter de Gruyter GmbH, Berlin/Boston, Genthiner Straße 13, 10785 Berlin
Illustrations: Happy Design
Coverdesign: Ion Jonas, Berlin
Typesetting: Integra Software Services Pvt. Ltd.

www.degruyterbrill.com
Questions about General Product Safety Regulation:
productsafety@degruyterbrill.com

Advance Praise

"*In the dynamic world of start-ups and scale-ups, intellectual property is often overlooked until it's too late. This book offers a refreshingly pragmatic and accessible guide to integrating IP into the strategic roadmap of growing ventures. What makes it particularly valuable is its direct relevance to founders and early-stage teams navigating the scale-up journey, investor conversations, and due diligence processes. By demystifying IP and anchoring it within the broader startup ecosystem—including funding, and acquisition readiness—it provides a critical toolset that too few early-stage entrepreneurs fully leverage. A must-read for anyone serious about building a secure and scalable business.*"
Omar Mohout—Scaleup Director, Deloitte

"*This book fills an important gap in the entrepreneurship literature. While innovation, business modelling, and IP rights in themselves are widely covered, there are few books connecting the dots between entrepreneurship, sustainable innovation, and intellectual property as clearly and practically as this guide does. I encourage students, entrepreneurs or managers to think early about their IP strategy—not just as a legal necessity, but as a tool for growth, value creation, and differentiation. This book is an excellent companion for that process: hands-on, easy to follow, and deeply relevant to the challenges early-stage innovators face.*"
Robin De Cock, PhD
Antwerp Management School
Associate Professor of Entrepreneurship
Academic director of the Master in Sustainable Innovation & Entrepreneurship
Co-founder of Antwerp Centre for Entrepreneurship Research

https://doi.org/10.1515/9783111673547-202

"I know An Cosaert as a highly driven, intelligent, and strategically sharp professional who not only understands the complex world of IP but also succeeds in conveying it in a particularly accessible and practice-oriented way. What makes this book so powerful is that An brings her wealth of experience with start-ups, scale-ups, and corporate venturing to life through clear examples and concrete methods that entrepreneurs can apply immediately. Her cases and practical tools show that IP is far more than just legal protection; it is a strategic instrument that provides direction, keeps your company agile, and unlocks growth opportunities. From my own career–spanning corporate innovations to mentoring young companies at Hangar K and iStart—I fully recognise how crucial this perspective is. That's why this book is a definite must-read for anyone looking to embed innovation in a sustainable and future-proof way."

Guy Van Wijmeersch
Founder White Space Strategic Design
Innovation Manager BOPLAN

"This book is an invaluable, down-to-earth guide for ambitious entrepreneurs. It opened my eyes to seeing intellectual property not as a dry legal box-ticking exercise, but as a powerful, strategic driver for growth. It made me realise that I don't need to protect everything—only what truly matters, but then do it properly and with foresight. Like our products, our IP strategy needs to grow and adapt over time. What really resonated with me is how clearly this book shows that true collaboration and sustainable scaling are only possible with a smart, integrated IP approach. I'd highly recommend it to any entrepreneur who wants to secure their innovation and unlock its full value for the future."

Johan Bonner—Co-founder Material Mastery

Contents

Disclaimer

This guide is not intended as legal advice. The author cannot be held liable if the information and recommendations contained in the guide are imprecise, inaccurate or no longer up-to-date. Nor does the author guarantee that the contents of this book will be applicable or relevant in all circumstances with regard to IP agreements. Each intellectual property measure, agreement or contractual clause must be adapted to the specific context in which it is concluded and comply with all applicable legal provisions. The author therefore recommends that users of the guide seek the assistance of a lawyer or legal expert when filing for intellectual property rights, drafting an agreement or contractual clause.

https://doi.org/10.1515/9783111673547-204

Author's note

My drive

Over the years, I have had the privilege of working with countless start-ups, scale-ups, and SMEs, each trying to navigate the complex and often misunderstood world of intellectual property (IP). During my interactions with young entrepreneurs, I have seen the same critical mistakes repeated time and again:

- **Confusing personal records with IP protection**
  Many entrepreneurs believe that simply writing down their ideas–whether in a notebook or elsewhere–automatically gives them ownership. While this might provide a sense of personal validation, it does not offer any legal protection. Without formal IP steps, ideas remain vulnerable to being developed independently by others.
- **Assuming an idea is completely new**
  Far too often, inventors assume their idea is completely new but do not take the time to check if something similar already exists. A good patent application should always start with a clear understanding of what is already out there. That way, you can be sure your invention is truly original.
- **Filing patents too quickly without thinking about return on investment**
  It is not uncommon to see patents rushed through that read more like general product descriptions rather than strong claims about the core innovation. If the claims are too narrow or vague, the patent might not offer much long-term value or support business growth.
- **Expecting patents alone to attract investors or buyers**
  There is a common belief that simply filing a patent will draw interest from investors. But patents usually are not published for about 18 months. If you are just waiting passively during that time, instead of actively reaching out to partners or investors, you could miss important opportunities.

These recurring mistakes highlight a deeper issue: When early-stage businesses think about IP at all, it is often in a reactive rather than a strategic way. While this is understandable, such a mindset leaves them unprepared for the broader dynamics of IP, especially in an international context where the rules of the game are often shaped by large corporations and long-established systems.

Today's management of intellectual property on a global scale remains focused on *protecting* ideas and innovations, often through strategies aimed at preventing infringement or preparing for potential litigation. This traditional approach continues to shape the IP service economy, particularly benefiting larger corpor-

https://doi.org/10.1515/9783111673547-205

ations with extensive resources. Those companies operate with well-established business models, which are unlikely to change significantly over time unless they engage in corporate venturing initiatives. Their significant budgets allow them to safeguard all protectable assets with comprehensive IP strategies.

In contrast, start-ups, scale-ups, and SMEs operate with limited budgets and dynamic business models, making traditional IP strategies less applicable. This underscores the need for a different approach–one better suited to smaller, fast-moving businesses.

For those companies we need to rethink traditional IP approaches and embrace a strategic mindset. Intellectual property rights are a tool, not an end goal. They should serve the broader purpose of supporting a scalable and sustainable business model. By aligning intellectual property strategies with business objectives, companies can maximise the value of their innovations and create long-term impact.

Over the years–driven by my passion for the intersection of innovation, entrepreneurship, and intellectual property–I have developed a unique perspective on how to secure and strengthen small businesses. As this perspective has proven valuable to many entrepreneurs, I felt compelled to share my practical insights–insights that can lead to well-informed decisions and concrete actions.

That is the main reason I decided to write this book. It is intended as a practical guide for start-ups, scale-ups, and SMEs, helping them make informed, strategic IP choices that support their growth ambitions and prepare their businesses for the challenges of the next five years and beyond.

How to use this book

Most books on intellectual property tell you what IP is and how to protect it–covering the different types and criteria of IP rights, the legal impact, and other key considerations. While this knowledge is essential, it is not enough.

This book takes a different approach. It is not just about understanding IP, it is about using IP strategically to fuel growth. Many start-ups, scale-ups and SMEs struggle to navigate IP because they do not have the vast resources of large corporations. They need IP to work for them, not against them–cost-effectively, practically, and in alignment with their business ambitions. This book, therefore, speaks the language of business first, and the language of IP second.

No worries though, we will start with a concise overview of IP and IP rights (IPR) to make sure that we are on the same page. But from there, this book will guide you through real-world business scenarios, helping you apply IP strategically to secure your ideas, strengthen your position, and scale your business effectively.

This book is not about protecting

For start-ups, scale-ups, and SMEs operating with limited budgets and evolving business models, IP should not be viewed as a legal shield. Instead, it can serve as a strategic business asset that creates room for growth over the next five years and beyond. In other words: IP is not just about protecting innovations; it is about using them to attract investors, strengthen market position, and generate long-term value.

This book shifts the perspective from defensive protection to building a future-proof business strategy. Rather than reacting to threats, you will learn how to take control and secure your business proactively–making smart, forward-thinking IP decisions that align with your business goals.

This book is not for corporates

If you are a multinational company with a well-established business model, you likely have the resources to register every possible IP asset, hire lawyers, and defend your position in court. This book is not for you.

This book is for small and growing businesses (typically less than 50 people) that operate more like speedboats than container ships. Speedboats are agile, fast, and innovative, but they also face high risks and turbulent waters. If you are navigating the fast-paced world of entrepreneurship, this book will help you steer your speedboat strategically–securing your business in a way that supports growth, rather than slowing you down.

Through case studies, practical tools and step-by-step strategies, you will learn how to make IP work for your business, even on a limited budget.

This book is not just about growing ideas

Many books address scalability as an afterthought. This book integrates scalability into every step of the business development process–helping you think strategically from the very beginning.

After all, ideas do not build business–strategy does. The real challenge is not coming up with innovative ideas; it is making sure that ideas can grow, scale, and succeed in a competitive landscape.

This book helps you:
- Develop a scalable concept from your initial idea
- Secure your concept with a future-proof, cost-effective IP strategy
- Anticipate potential challenges before they arise
- Leverage IP to attract investment, partnerships, and growth opportunities

What this book is about

This book is about empowering entrepreneurs with the knowledge and tools to make strategic, cost-effective IP decisions that drive business growth.

Start-ups, scale-ups, and SMEs often find themselves at a disadvantage in the IP landscape. While large corporations can afford expensive, all-encompassing IP strategies, smaller businesses need smart, targeted approaches that align with their resources and goals.

This book bridges this gap, offering practical, real-world guidance tailored to the unique challenges of growing businesses.

It provides:
- Actionable insights to help you secure your business without overspending
- Cost-effective methods for IP due diligence and strategic decision-making
- A shift in mindset-from defensive IP protection to proactive business security
- A roadmap to transform ideas into thriving, scalable enterprises

This book raises awareness about the strategic value IP can bring to your business. Based on 30 years of practical experience, this book is designed to set you on the right path. It is not an exhaustive guide, as every business is unique. I strongly encourage you to seek professional advice, but above all, understand what IP means within your company and recognise how you can leverage it for growth.

While the principles in this book are broadly applicable, it is especially valuable for businesses in:
- technology and software
- biotech and healthcare
- consumer products and manufacturing
- any industry where innovation and agility are competitive advantages

Though my expertise is rooted in European IP management, most insights apply globally, certainly in regions with a dynamic start-up ecosystem.

You can read this book from cover to cover, but you do not have to. Depending on:
- your familiarity with IP: Have you already filed a trademark or patent, or is this the first time?
- the stage of your business: Are you already selling products? Or are you still building your start-up?
- the specific IP challenges you are facing: Are you hiring and do you need to know how IP is handled in employment or collaboration contracts? Are you facing IP issues with third parties?

Or you can jump between chapters and apply the insights that matter most to you. However, the order is not entirely random. We first explore how to build a solid speedboat business, and then how to secure it for sustainable growth.

Throughout this book, you will find:
- case studies illustrating the best (and worst) ways to apply IP strategy
- practical methods and tools to help you make informed decisions
- a glossary and reading list for deeper exploration

Use this book as a practical guide for key actions throughout your speedboat journey:
- quickly verifying necessary steps when something new arises, such as hiring your first crew
- defining relevant IPR
- fostering collaboration and embrace innovation as a team
- recognising the value of IP as an intangible asset for your company
- establishing a data room from the very beginning
- preparing for IP due diligence and ensure your business is investment-ready

Think of this book as a manual–a tool you can refer back to whenever you need clarity. If your copy ends up with dog-eared pages and notes, I will know I have done my job . . .

Chapter 1
Speedboat business

https://doi.org/10.1515/9783111673547-001

1.0 Introduction

What to expect

- Understand why a small business is a speedboat
- What characteristics lead to this designation
- Understand how these characteristics affect the security of the business

In 2023, I attended the Innov8rs conference in Lisbon, focused on corporate venturing–where large companies create start-up-like teams to enhance intrapreneurship and to explore new business models, products, or services with greater agility and freedom. During a session on IP, moderated by Frank Mattes, we discussed the challenges these intrapreneurial teams face, in particular the clash between the need to experiment and move fast and the parent companies' rigid IP framework.

As I listened, I realised these challenges mirror those of the start-ups, scale-ups, and SMEs I have been working with. In both cases, limited resources demand strategic choices that prioritise growth. A common metaphor in corporate venturing compares these teams to speedboats, manoeuvring nimbly while their parent companies act as container ships.

The speedboat metaphor resonated with me. It perfectly captures the agility, risk-taking, and strategic decision-making that define small companies. It also provides the ideal framework for this book, which is structured into five parts:

1. First, we explore some fundamentals of IP and IP rights and the defining characteristics of a speedboat business–both essential building blocks for the chapters ahead.
2. With these foundations in place, we can now focus on how to build a resilient, high-performing business.
3. Next, we dive into securing this business, showing how to harness innovation and entrepreneurial spirit through using IP as a strategic asset for growth.
4. In Chapter 4, we address what happens when your speedboat business is running at full speed and needs funding–while maximising the return on your innovations and IP investments.
5. Finally, we wrap up with a case study, summarising key takeaways and how to apply them in practice.

1.1 The basics of IP and IPR

Understanding intellectual property and intellectual property rights is essential for building and scaling your speedboat business. This overview covers the fundamental concepts you need to get started, helping you secure and leverage your IP assets.

For a deeper dive into specific topics, check Chapter 3 and the reading list. If you are looking for additional IP-related terms beyond these basics, check out the glossary.

IP vs IPR

Though both terms are often used interchanged, there is a clear difference between IP and IPR.

Intellectual Property or IP refers to creations of the human intellect–such as inventions, designs, symbols, names, artistic works, software, and trade secrets. In a business context, IP also encompasses the know-how, including trade secrets, that underpins the development of these creations and the contractual agreements put in place to secure both the know-how and the resulting innovations.

These creations can become valuable assets, a measure to secure these assets is by applying intellectual property rights.

Intellectual Property Rights or IPR are the legal rights granted to the creators or owners of IP for a limited period of time and within a specific region. These rights enable them to benefit from their intellectual creations by excluding others from using their innovations without permission and by allowing them to commercialise their innovations.

The core principle of IP is that it transforms intangible creations–such as an idea, invention, or brand name–into assets with legal protections. IPR incentivises innovation through ensuring that creators can benefit financially from their work while preventing unauthorised use by others.

Types of IPR

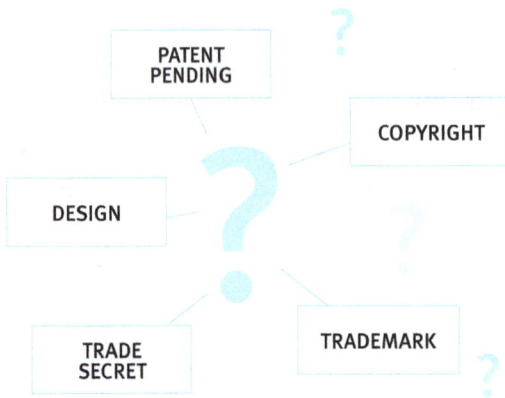

Though people primarily associate IPR with patents, there are several categories of protection for different types of IP, e.g.:
- **patents:** for new inventions
- **trademarks:** for distinctive brand names, logos, slogans, and the like
- **copyrights:** for original works of authorship like music, books, and software
- **industrial designs:** for the visual appearance of products
- **trade secrets:** for confidential business information that gives a company a competitive advantage, such as formulas, processes, or customer lists.

These elements are explained in detail in Chapter 3 where the boat's construction is explored.

IP management vs IP strategy

IP management encompasses the day-to-day measures needed to safeguard and maintain intellectual property. IP strategy, on the other hand, focuses on the broader decisions that underpin business growth.
IP management involves:
- **identification:** spotting and applying for relevant IPR
- **filing and registration:** ensuring each identified IP right is properly filed and follows all necessary procedures for official grant or registration
- **monitoring and enforcement:** keeping a close eye on competitors' IP activities, addressing infringement, and taking legal action when necessary
- **maintenance:** preserving protection by following renewal requirements and other procedures

- **licensing and contracts:** managing IP sales, license agreements, and dedicated IP contracts.

IP strategy, on the other hand, involves:
- **IP portfolio strategy:** choosing which IP assets are vital to your business goals and need to be developed or acquired
- **competitive positioning:** using IP to differentiate offerings, shape markets, and deter competition
- **monetisation:** exploring licensing, sales, or partnerships to generate return on your IP
- **market and innovation strategy:** integrating IP into product development, innovation, and market coverage

IP strategy–like the speedboat's navigation system–is explained in Chapter 3. For a deeper look into IP management, see the sections in the same chapter on people, construction, and the ecosystem.

Key IPR mechanisms

There are various IPR mechanisms to protect and leverage IP. To secure your intellectual property effectively, it is essential to follow a well-structured, consistent process for filing and monitoring each registration–whether it concerns a trademark, design right, or patent.

The key mechanisms outlined below apply to all types of IPR and must be understood and observed at every step:
- **date stamp:** Timing is everything when it comes to IP. To avoid discussion about who was first (in terms of patents) or when something was created (in terms of copyright), it is crucial that you make sure you are able to prove the exact date of creation.
- **registration:** In many cases, IPR are established through a formal registration process. For example, patents, trademarks, and industrial designs require applications to be filed with relevant authorities. This process ensures that the creator's rights are legally recognised and enforceable. Copyright is automatically granted upon creation, but you can register it for extra protection.
- **exclusive rights:** Once granted, IPR provide exclusivity. This means owners have the legal authority to decide how their IP is used, whether that involves commercialising, licensing, or restricting others from copying or reproducing it.

- **duration:** IPR are not forever. This ensures a balance between incentivising innovation and allowing others to build upon older ideas over time.
  Per type of IP, different periods of legal protection apply, e.g.:
  - Patents: typically last 20 years
  - Trademarks: can be renewed indefinitely
  - Copyright: typically lasts the creator's lifetime plus 50–70 years
- **enforcement**: If someone uses your IP without permission, IPR can be enforced through legal action. This requires clear evidence of ownership and, in some cases, proof of unauthorised use or infringement.

More details on IPR mechanisms can be found in Chapter 3, which delves into the speedboat's construction elements.

1.2 The characteristics of a speedboat business

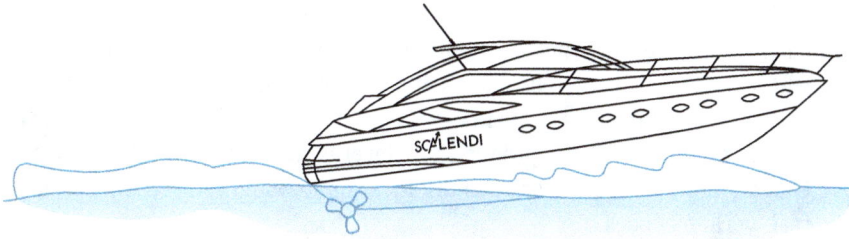

Speedboat businesses are defined by key characteristics such as:
- small and agile
- vision and goals
- autonomy and empowerment
- rapid prototyping and iteration
- risk-taking and experimenting
- faster decision-making
- focus on market and customer needs
- efficiency and resource optimisation
- flexibility and adaptability
- collaboration

Many of these characteristics are also common in start-ups, scale-ups, and SMEs. These smaller businesses naturally operate like speedboats, though they may not realise how this analogy can help them structure and strengthen their operations. Let us take a closer look at how these elements apply.
- **Small and agile**
  Start-ups, scale-ups, and SMEs often have lean teams, which makes them flexible and responsive. They are still searching for the right business model and the ideal customer, but this small scale allows them to pivot quickly when needed.
- **Vision and goals**
  While many small businesses focus on short-term survival–earning enough to thrive–developing a clear vision and long-term goals is key. These will guide the company towards building a sustainable and scalable business, as we will discuss in the next chapter.

- **Autonomy and empowerment**
  Smaller businesses have the advantage of independence. Founders are typically passionate about their products and services, inspiring their teams to embrace the journey wholeheartedly. This autonomy creates an environment where bold decisions can be made without reliance on external structures.
- **Rapid prototyping and iteration**
  Creating minimum viable products and leveraging tools like the Lean Startup Canvas, allow small businesses to test ideas quickly and refine them based on real-world feedback.
- **Risk-taking and experimenting**
  Small businesses are fearless. They launch products or services without waiting for perfection, test new business models, experiment with networks, and push forward with conviction in their unique selling propositions.
- **Faster decision-making**
  The combination of drive, passion, and a willingness to take risks allows these businesses to make swift decisions. They learn fast, adapt quickly, and iterate often, keeping pace with changing circumstances.
- **Focus on market and customer needs**
  Start-ups, scale-ups, and SMEs excel in customer centricity. They focus their entire strategy on understanding their customers and markets, often identifying and addressing latent needs before others do.
- **Efficiency and resource optimisation**
  With tight budgets, limited time, and small teams, these businesses are masters at doing more with less. Collaboration and playing to each team member's strengths are key to maintaining efficiency and achieving goals.
- **Flexibility and adaptability**
  Business models and customer targets are rarely set in stone. These companies are open to change, adapting quickly when the original plan does not work out.
- **Collaboration**
  Start-ups, scale-ups, and SMEs thrive on networks. They collaborate with larger companies interested in their solutions and learn from peers within entrepreneurial ecosystems, sharing knowledge and resources along the way.

1.3 Speedboat challenges that need securing

These speedboat business characteristics present challenges when developing an IP strategy for scalable growth.

– **Adaptability vs IP boundaries**
  IPR require clear boundaries of protection, which can be problematic if changes are needed after filing. Will adjustments still be safe to implement? Will the protection scope remain valid?
– **Speed vs protection**
  The drive for rapid market introduction often leads start-ups to go public before securing IP, risking, e.g., unintended disclosure or loosing patent opportunities.
– **Customer centricity vs scalability**
  In their rush to reach customers quickly, start-ups often overlook the fact that they are still in the development phase. Prioritising the needs of a specific customer may, in turn, hinder their ability to scale rapidly into other markets.
– **Speedboats vs container ships**
  Partnering with large corporations that have strong IP strategies and vast IP budgets can put start-ups at a disadvantage. In their eagerness to collaborate, they may overlook critical IP measures.

What experience shows is that when speedboat businesses think ahead and focus on securing their IP with the next five years in mind, their IP strategy naturally keeps up with change and secures what really matters. That is why this book puts strong emphasis on using IP to drive sustainable growth.

1.4 The key components of a speedboat

Let us first break down the composition of a speedboat business into its core elements, and then proceed to see how each of these can connect to a successful IP and growth strategy.

The three crucial elements that determine whether your speedboat business can truly excel:

– **People**

Every successful speedboat needs an entrepreneurial captain, a capable crew, and trusted supporters from the shore. Founders, employees, mentors, strategic partners, et cetera all play a role in steering the speedboat through ever-changing conditions.

– **Construction**

Just like a well-engineered speedboat, a business relies on its fundamental structure. Every part–whether the hull, the engine, or the navigation system–must work in harmony to ensure high-performance, resilience, and adaptability.

– **Ecosystem**

Your speedboat does not operate in isolation. Market conditions, competitors, regulations, economic trends, et cetera all act like the ocean, other vessels, and the ever-changing weather, influencing every decision you make on your journey to success.

Wrapping up

Now that you understand why small businesses operate like nimble speedboats and how this influences the development of an IP strategy, you are ready to start building and securing your own speedboat business.

The next chapter will guide you through how to build your speedboat. After all, you cannot secure something that has not been properly built. Then, in Chapter 3, we will explore concrete steps to secure the speedboat business you have built.

Chapter 2
Build your speedboat business

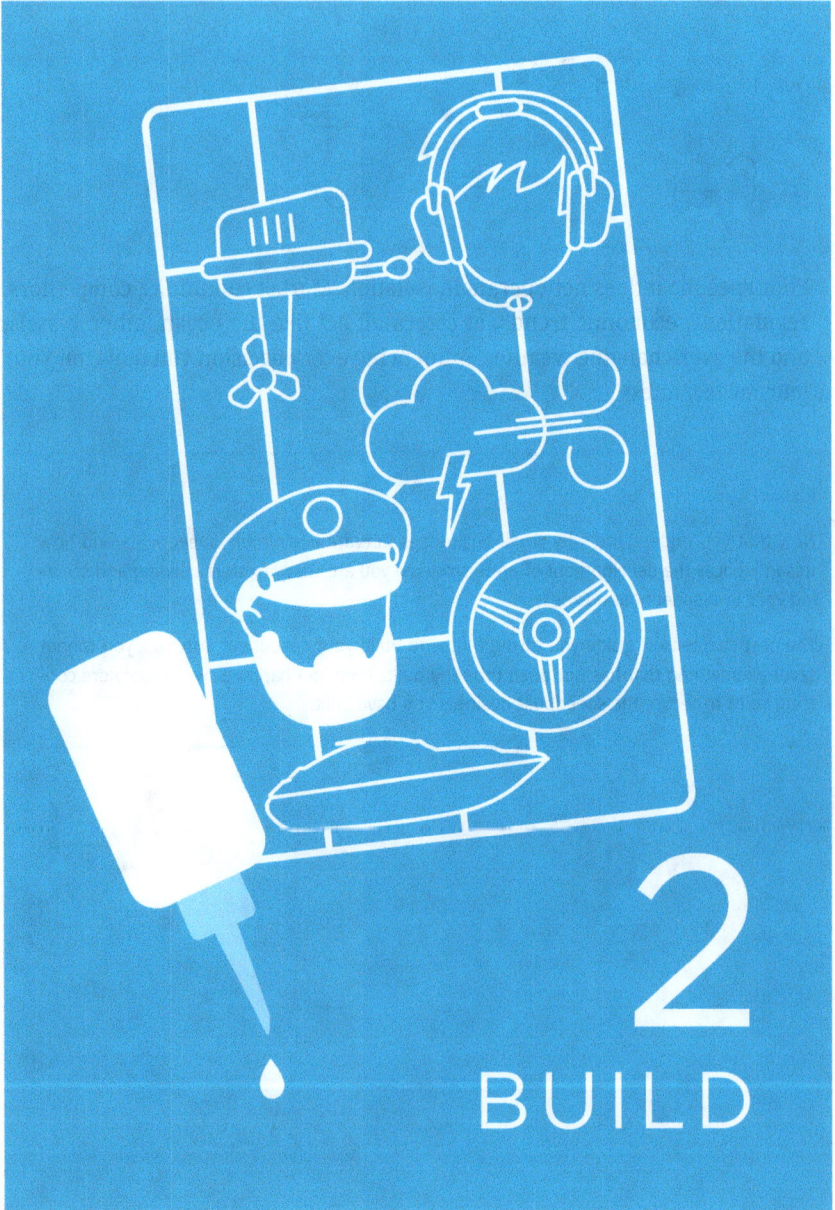

2
BUILD

https://doi.org/10.1515/9783111673547-002

2.0 Introduction

> **What to expect**
>
> In this chapter, you will learn to:
> – build a robust, manoeuvrable boat by weaving innovation and entrepreneurship into every aspect
> – ensure ongoing agility so it remains responsive for at least the next five years

Running a start-up, scale-up or SME is much like navigating a speedboat. Unlike large corporations–often compared to container ships, slow to turn–small businesses are fast, agile, and highly responsive to their environment. They can pivot quickly in response to new opportunities, adapt rapidly to market changes, and experiment with innovative strategies without being slowed down by bureaucracy. Looking at small businesses through this speedboat metaphor helps clarify how agility and responsiveness can become strategic advantages.

However, speed alone is not sufficient for success. The construction of the boat itself is equally critical; its sleek hull, powerful engine, and high-quality fuel determine how effectively and reliably it performs. Just as important are the people steering and maintaining the speedboat, as their skills ensure smooth and effective sailing.

To transform your business into a robust, scalable enterprise, all the key parts of your speedboat–**people, construction, and ecosystem**–must work seamlessly together. Your business must withstand rough waters and continue moving forward, even under pressure. This requires a clear and refined business model, optimised operations, and a strategic focus on sustainable growth.

Yet, even the strongest boat needs safeguarding. Security only becomes valuable when there is truly something worth protecting: a thriving, well-built enterprise designed to last. That is why, before addressing how to secure your business (the topic we will cover in Chapter 3), it is essential first to establish a solid foundation.

This chapter, therefore, zooms in on the building blocks of your speedboat business and explains how to create a resilient, high-performing company. Every successful venture begins with its captain, so we will first explore the critical roles played by the people involved. Once you understand who is on board and why they matter, we will delve into the boat's construction–discovering what makes it both agile and robust. Finally, we will look at the broader ecosystem, providing insight into how your speedboat can navigate external forces with confidence.

2.1 People

People are the foundation of any business. Their expertise, vision, and skills bring ideas to life, transforming potential into a thriving venture. A great idea is not enough, it needs a solid business model, a defined market, and the right customers–but most of all it requires capable hands to steer it forward.

Building a speedboat business is never a solo journey. Success comes through collaboration, diverse perspectives, and mutual trust, creating the conditions for sustainable growth and resilience.

When considering the people on board of a speedboat, it naturally begins with the **captain**–the one who takes the initiative to turn an innovative idea into a business. As the speedboat grows and becomes harder to steer alone, the captain brings in a **crew**. Eventually, additional **support** becomes essential to drive further growth.

Captain

Having a great idea is only the first step. To unlock its potential and turn it into a thriving speedboat business, it needs a captain–an entrepreneur with the vision, determination, and skills to navigate competitive waters. Many inventors have brilliant ideas, but only those who can transform them into profitable businesses truly take the helm of their speedboat.

Much like the boat's captain, a founder or CEO steers the business, setting its direction, speed, and course corrections. His vision and perseverance determine whether the speedboat can navigate obstacles, seize opportunities, and reach its destination.

Key skills

To be an effective captain, certain skills are key:

Problem-solving
Captains must swiftly identify challenges, use their expertise, skills and the latest technology at their disposal, and think outside the box to come up with effective–albeit unconventional–solutions to customer needs.

Adaptability
Launching a solution does not guarantee immediate success. Captains must adjust to feedback, refine their product, and pivot when necessary to stay on course. Early detection of market shifts and customer needs is critical.

Resilience
Obstacles are inevitable. Captains who embrace setbacks as learning opportunities build not only stronger businesses but also sharper entrepreneurial instincts. Some companies take years to succeed–persistence is key.

Industry awareness

Skilled captains understand the waters they navigate. Knowing market trends, competitor movements, and industry shifts helps founders position their business effectively and create real value.

Beyond traditional networking

No journey is taken alone. Strong captains actively seek diverse perspectives by stepping outside their comfort zone. While many founders network within their industry's circles, unexpected insights often come from unrelated fields.

How shoes solved my polymer puzzle

While working in R&D, I encountered a significant challenge: bonding polymers effectively under extreme weather conditions. Conventional adhesives failed to do the trick. After exhausting options within my own field, I broadened my search and discovered an unexpected source of inspiration: the shoe industry.

It turned out shoemakers had long tackled similar issues, developing specialised adhesives capable of withstanding harsh environments and continuous stress. By applying insights from their approach, we solved our polymer-bonding problem–an innovation breakthrough that would have been impossible if I had stayed within my own industry.

This experience taught me the immense value of looking beyond familiar boundaries to fresh solutions. Innovation often thrives at the intersection of different industries, where unconventional ideas unlock extraordinary results.

Crew

As a business grows, the speedboat becomes too large and complex to navigate alone. A captain sets the course, but no journey succeeds through leadership alone. Building a strong, engaged crew–one that shares the captain's vision and is prepared for the challenges ahead–is essential.

A well-balanced crew brings diverse expertise, maturity, and adaptability, ensuring the speedboat stays agile. In a fast-changing environment, frequent manoeuvring and course corrections are necessary, and having a crew that embraces the ride makes all the difference. Start-ups, scale-ups, and SMEs need team members who are not just skilled but genuinely committed to the mission.

Beyond hiring the right people, retaining and engaging them is equally crucial. As Jim Collins highlights in *Good to Great:*[1]

> *If people join the bus primarily because of where it is going, what happens if you get ten miles down the road and you need to change direction? You've got a problem. But if people are on the bus because of who else is on the bus, then it's much easier to change direction. Second, if you have the right people on the bus, the problem of how to motivate and manage people largely goes away.*

When crew members feel ownership of their roles, they step up when needed, keeping the speedboat running smoothly and at full speed.

Crew diversity

Even more important, however, is assembling the right combination of people. It is not simply about individual expertise, but how those individual strengths blend to form a cohesive, well-balanced team. One person might bring creativity, another

---

1 Collins, J. (2010). *Good to Great*, Business Contact.

technical excellence–and together, they can develop solutions neither would have found alone. Creating synergy within your crew means achieving outcomes where the whole is genuinely greater than the sum of its parts.

To achieve this synergy, certain characteristics and dynamics are particularly valuable for a speedboat business. Ideally, your team should blend complementary knowledge, skills, and innovation mindsets. Early on, this might involve bringing in (part-time) expert freelancers who help accelerate development while keeping your operations lean.

When assembling your crew, strive for a mix of innovation profiles:
- **ideators**, who constantly generate new ideas
- **analysts**, who excel at critical evaluation
- **implementers**, who are focused on quick execution and tangible progress
- **generalists**, who connect the dots, translating ideas into a viable business plan

This diverse crew ensures your speedboat business maintains the optimal balance between creativity, analysis, and swift action, laying the foundation for sustained success.

Lessons from a team challenge

During a workshop on innovation maturity, participants with similar profiles were grouped. Each group was asked to organise the yearly company incentive within a limited time. The results perfectly illustrated the importance of having a mix of profiles on board:
- The ideators spent the entire time listing bold ideas without considering feasibility.
- The analysts were paralysed by a lack of information and barely got started.
- The implementers dove straight into execution, without even considering what the incentive should be.

Key skills

Beyond their innovation profiles, a successful speedboat crew shares certain key skills.

Adaptability and flexibility
Start-ups rarely follow a straight path. Unexpected challenges require constant adjustments. A team that embraces change can deftly manoeuvre these challenges and maintain speed.

Entrepreneurial mindset

Crew members do not need to be founders or shareholders, but they should act as if they own the company. Crew members with a sense of ownership take initiative, solve problems proactively, and are willing to contribute far beyond their job descriptions.

Resourcefulness

In early-stage businesses, resources are often limited. A resourceful crew finds innovative solutions, maximises efficiency, and turns constraints into opportunities. Look for crew members with a track record of making the most of what's available.

Budget vs scalability

When building your crew, it is key to balance short-term needs and actions with long-term scalability and sustainability. Full-time employees provide stability, but freelancers offer flexibility and specialised expertise without long-term commitments.

In early stages, hiring freelancers for technical expertise can help build your minimum viable product faster. Once traction is gained, assembling a permanent team ensures sustainable growth.

Growth potential

A successful crew is not just skilled, it grows with your business. As your speedboat scales, crew members should adapt to evolving responsibilities, stepping into leadership roles when needed.

People who see clear growth opportunities within your company are more likely to stay committed, take ownership, and drive long-term success.

Support

While a strong crew is essential, navigating challenging waters often requires extra expertise. This is where support–external resources, networks, and partnerships–comes into play.

The right support can help you make faster, better-informed decisions, solve problems efficiently, and remain competitive in a fast-paced world. Building a speedboat business is not just about bringing a crew on board; it is also about leveraging collaboration and open innovation.

We live in a time of rapid change and growing complexity, where collaboration is no longer optional–it is essential for driving progress and achieving meaningful results. Speedboat businesses need both speed and agility–qualities that external support can provide.

Support takes many forms, including:

Structural support

Structural support encompasses essential services that form the foundation of a stable and well-functioning business.
– **Strategy consultants:** help define mission and vision and outline goals and KPIs
– **Accounting and finance experts**: ensure accurate bookkeeping, tax compliance, and financial planning
– **IP strategists, IP officers, legal advisors**: handle contracts, secure IP, and guide you through regulatory requirements
– **Marketing specialists**: build brand awareness, engage target audiences, and generate demand
– **HR consultants**: support recruitment, employee management, and contractual matters

Mentors

Mentors are mature, experienced individuals who act as guides and soundboards throughout your business journey. Whether you find them through personal networks, incubators, or accelerators, mentors provide invaluable strategic input.

Think of them as experienced fellow captains standing on the shore or occasionally boarding your speedboat, offering advice when needed. They focus on your business as a whole rather than product or process specifics, making their insights particularly valuable in early-stage growth.

The value of mentors:
- They share industry experience to help you avoid pitfalls.
- They provide access to valuable networks, opening doors to opportunities and resources.
- They offer motivation, encouragement, and perspective in stormy weather.
- They hold you accountable, ensuring progress and strategic alignment.

A mentor who believes in and supports your business can be an incredible source of confidence and growth, helping both captain and crew stay focused, even in rough waters.

Contractors

Hiring contractors–whether individuals, companies, or institutions–can enhance specific elements of your product or process.

For example:
- **Design firms** can refine your product's shape, improving performance, overall attractiveness, and functionality.
- **IT professionals** can create custom code to enhance system efficiency and robustness, strengthen digital infrastructure, cybersecurity, and technological efficiency.
- **(Technical) universities and research centres** can provide access to cutting-edge innovations and insights on disruptive forces.

By working with contractors, your business benefits from specialised skills without needing to develop everything in-house, enabling you to move faster by skipping learning curves.

Innovation does not always mean starting from scratch. Leveraging existing technology–a strategy known as **licensing** technology–allows businesses to integrate proven solutions rather than reinvent the wheel. This can significantly accelerate innovation and growth, while reducing development time, costs, and risks. Contractors with access to licensed technology can speed up implementation and help your speedboat business stay agile and competitive.

> **Tip**
>
> As a small business, choosing whether to seek support is entirely up to you. However, in today's fast-moving world, it is nearly impossible for a small team to keep up with every new technology, market shift, or regulatory change.
>
> Even if you are a tech start-up working on cutting-edge innovation–such as artificial intelligence–external support can help you address the complexities of scaling, securing funding, and managing partnerships.
>
> By leveraging the right support, your speedboat gains the agility, strength, and resilience it needs to accelerate towards success.

2.2 Construction

Once you have ensured strong leadership, assembled the right crew and secured external support, the next step is to build the speedboat itself. Just as a captain and crew depend on a well-constructed vessel to navigate unpredictable waters, your business needs a solid foundation with carefully designed systems that ensure performance, adaptability, and scalability.

To launch a successful speedboat business, every component must be crafted with precision, ensuring that all elements work together to maximise efficiency. Understanding how these components interact is key to unlocking the full potential of your business.

The boat as a whole represents your product or service–once you are on a roll, you can have multiple boats. The **hull** of your boat is the visible, tangible aspect, attracting customers and other stakeholders. The **engine** is the powerhouse, while the **navigation system** ensures strategic direction and control. And of course, the right **fuel** ensures that your boat reaches cruising speed.

In the following sections we will explore these critical construction elements in detail, illustrating how they help transform an initial idea into a thriving, scalable enterprise.

Hull

The hull represents the visible, tangible aspect of your business, the first impression customers have of your product or service. A strong hull is attractive, functional, and designed with customers in mind.

While incremental updates or adjustments can enhance its efficiency, a poorly designed hull will ultimately undermine your entire business. Prioritising **customer centricity** ensures that the hull is both visually appealing and structurally sound.

A hull designed to meet customer needs creates the ideal streamline, allowing your speedboat to glide smoothly and pivot with ease. With minimal friction, it can move fast, adapt quickly, respond to customer feedback, and make subtle adjustments to gain greater traction in shifting markets.

In contrast, poor customer centricity–or a poorly optimised streamline–can slow your progress and drain energy. Without a clear focus on the customer, your speedboat business risks reacting too slowly and losing its edge in a fast-paced, competitive environment.

To stay ahead, businesses often adopt **a minimum viable product (MVP)** approach to test new products and services. By launching early and iterating based on real-world feedback, your speedboat business becomes better aligned with customer needs.

This ability to experiment, test, and adapt is essential for any start-up or scale-up. Early input from customers can be invaluable, and long-term success often depends on how quickly and effectively you respond to changing circumstances. This level of agility requires a sharp focus and a well-designed hull–so choose wisely.

One effective approach to achieve a performant hull, is **design thinking**. Design thinking integrates:
- **customer needs**: understanding what people truly want
- **technological possibilities**: leveraging innovations for better solutions
- **business viability**: ensuring sustainable growth

Design thinking: Innovate with empathy

Design thinking is a dynamic, human-centred approach to problem-solving that helps businesses deeply understand their customers and environment. By emphasising empathy, collaboration, and experimentation, it drives innovative solutions and customer-centric growth.

Using visual tools like canvasses, design thinking offers a structured yet flexible framework to navigate complex systems. It shifts the focus from internal processes to real customer needs, ensuring relevance and impact.

The Double Diamond Approach

A key methodology within design thinking, the Double Diamond–developed by the British Design Council–guides innovation through four phases

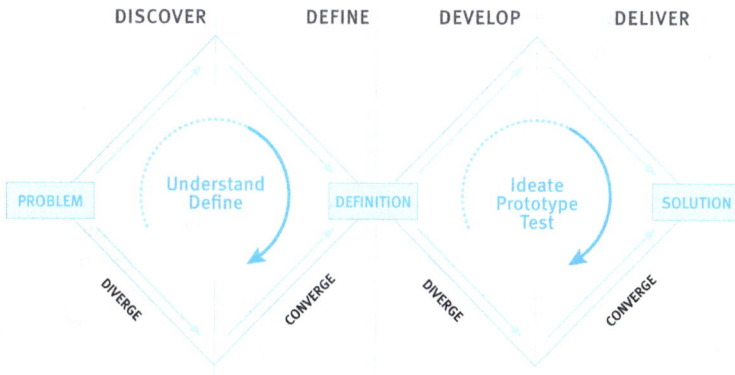

- Discover: Gather insights, explore challenges, and identify opportunities.
- Define: Sharpen focus by clearly articulating the core problem.
- Develop: Brainstorm, prototype, and test creative solutions.
- Deliver: Refine and implement the best solution.

Named for its two diverging and converging phases, the Double Diamond expands possibilities before narrowing in on the optimal outcome. This ensures that your business's "hull" is not only attractive but deeply aligned with customer needs.

Engine

While the hull attracts customers, the invisible engine is the powerhouse of your business: the systems and technologies that keep everything running behind the scenes. This includes:
- the software powering a vision system
- the control systems managing a device
- the mechanisms that open and close components
- the equipment to produce your materials
- the machinery involved in food production
- . . .

An engine is a complex system, composed of multiple interdependent subparts. Some subparts are directly customer-related, while others ensure the overall functionality and efficiency of the engine.

A strong business engine typically consists of:
- **operational mechanisms**: the internal system that drives performance
- **technology and processes**: the backbone of product or service delivery
- **scalability mechanisms**: ensuring sustainable, long-term growth

Many small businesses, in their early stages, focus solely on getting things up and running without properly structuring their engine. However, taking the time to document your engine is essential. Clearly defining each component and its function, and registering the reasoning behind design choices will prove invaluable as your business grows.

Keeping your speedboat at peak performance

Just like an engine requires regular maintenance, your business requires continuous refinement to stay competitive. Performance monitoring and proactive adjustments ensure your speedboat remains agile, efficient and ready for new challenges.

By integrating customer feedback and business insights, you can tweak your engine and prevent inefficiencies before they slow you down. Monitoring tools–like sensors or data checkpoints–help track performance and detect early warning signs. In today's data-driven world, information is gold. Capturing and analysing the right data enables smarter decision-making and enhances long-term resilience.

Adapting to emerging technologies is equally crucial. Ignoring new developments means risking stagnation, while smart integration can give your business a competitive advantage. Instead of overhauling your entire system when a new disruptive technology arises, treat your engine as a modular system–testing and refining small components separately before integrating them. This approach minimises downtime and reduces risk.

Sustainable success lies in treating your engine as a living system–one that evolves along with business insights, customer feedback, and technological advancements. The businesses that thrive are those that optimise and adapt, ensuring their speedboat remains ahead of the fleet, no matter how turbulent the waters.

Staying ahead with exponential thinking

In today's world, where new technologies evolve at exponential speed and redefine entire industries, businesses must be proactive in preparing for change. A key approach to cope with this rapid evolution is exponential thinking. This approach involves continuously scanning the horizon for emerging technologies and considering how they might affect or benefit your business.

The key is to stay connected with research centres, universities, and innovation hubs to observe, learn, and translate new discoveries into potential business models before they become mainstream. Groundbreaking research often remains hidden in laboratories for years before reaching commercial maturity. Staying ahead of these developments enables you to ride the wave of innovation, or even become the wave yourself.

A few examples of early research that eventually transforms industries:
- After graduating in the early 1990s, I started working on textile composites at the KU Leuven materials research centre MTM. At the time, most industries were unfamiliar with composites and their potential applications. My research focused on how knitted and woven textiles, in particular 3D textiles, could reinforce composite materials. Nearly 20 years later, when working as an innovation advisor, I came across a company that was seen as highly innovative for using 3D woven composites. It had taken two decades to refine the technology and make it both economically and technologically viable.
- In 1996, while working at the international development centre of Recticel, we experimented with neural networks to scan and classify foam structures in collaboration with the Fraunhofer Institute. This is now considered cutting-edge artificial intelligence, but it was already being researched 30 years ago.

Fuel

Hull and engine are useless without fuel. If you do not have the right fuel or run out of fuel, you can either not leave the harbour or get stuck in the middle of the ocean. Fuel is the lifeline of your speedboat business, ensuring that you have the necessary resources to move forward, adapt, and grow.

This fuel is your know-how. Just as fuel powers a vehicle, know-how fuels your business–enabling quick decisions, product iterations, and strategic pivots. Without the right know-how, a business can stall or lose direction.

In speedboat businesses, know-how goes beyond technical skills; it includes insight into market trends, customer needs, and efficient ways of working.

The more robust and adaptable your know-how, the better equipped your business is to innovate and grow. In short: fuel is know-how, a constant, reliable resource that keeps your business moving forward.

An essential part of your know-how is your data:
- customer and supplier insights
- market and tend analysis
- product development and product performance
- process and operational data

As is often said, data is the new gold, and it holds crucial value for your business. As a young company, you can never collect too much data; you never know what might turn out to be useful or strategically important in the future.

Thus, your know-how is key:
- **The more** you know about your customer, the better you can design the hull of your boat.
- **The more** you know about your product, the more efficient you can build your engine.
- **The more** you know about your market and competition, the faster you can navigate your boat.

Fuel additives: leveraging an "unfair advantage"

Just as fuel can enhance its performance with specific additives, so too can your know-how benefit from that extra information, that additional angle of analysis, that deeper insight.

Every speedboat business has a unique background–shaped by the captain, the crew, or both–that influences its approach to problem-solving. In marketing, this is often called an **unfair advantage**, though *fair* advantage might be more accurate, as there is nothing wrong with leveraging your unique experiences to create something others cannot easily replicate.

Your personal journey–whether shaped by passion, education, or work–can offer insights that set your business apart. Recognising and embracing this unfair advantage is key to navigating competitive waters with confidence and positioning your business for success.

Unfair advantage: a competitive advantage or a risk?

An unfair advantage gives an individual or entity a disproportionate edge over others–often due to exclusive access, insider knowledge, or unique resources not available to everyone.

In this context, the unfair advantage is drawn from the captain or one of his crew members, who possesses unique skills, knowledge, or relationships that give the speedboat business a competitive advantage.

– **Unique expertise and skills**
   Technical expertise, industry-specific knowledge, highly creative problem-solving abilities, et cetera can make all the difference. A specialist in AI, a seasoned product designer, or an industry veteran can drive innovation and problem-solving beyond what competitors can achieve.
– **Strategic relationships and networks**
   Connections with key investors, clients, or industry leaders can open doors that others struggle to access. A well-respected captain with an impressive track record can also boost the company's credibility.
– **Cultural and intellectual capital**
   Unique perspectives, deep market understanding, and adaptive thinking can shape a company's ability to develop and scale innovative products or services.

When the individual's skills or insights are deeply embedded in a company's identity, they become a defining factor in its market success.

An unfair advantage rooted in individual talent can be a powerful driver of innovation and market leadership. However, to turn this into lasting success, businesses must capture and share that knowledge, ensuring their competitive advantage does not rely on one person alone. If key knowledge is not documented, it can be lost in the event of sudden illness or departure, putting the business at risk.

From maintaining machines to redefining them

Before starting his business, an entrepreneur spent years as a maintenance engineer specialising in construction machinery. He became an expert in solving recurring maintenance issues, making improvements, and identifying inefficiencies.

Drawing on this experience, he launched his own company to design more efficient, high-performance machines. In no time, he managed to capture a significant share of the market.

His expertise as maintenance engineer became his unfair advantage.

Navigation system

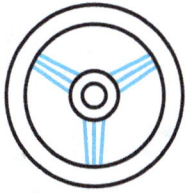

A strong speedboat does not just rely on an attractive hull, a powerful engine or the right fuel–it also needs a robust navigation system to stay on course and help you achieve your vision and mission.

A boat, no matter how well-built or well-equipped, needs a clear **destination**–a long-term goal that goes beyond simply serving customers. This broader ambition is captured in your **mission and vision:**
- **mission:** defines your business's purpose–what you do, for whom, and why it matters
- **vision:** looks ahead, outlining what your business aims to achieve in a changing world

Together, they act as a compass, guiding strategic decisions and enabling sustainable growth.

In a fast-paced world, a vision and mission alone are often not enough to survive. Today's societal challenges–reflected in the **Sustainable Development Goals (SDG's)**–call for higher aims. By defining your Massive Transformative Purpose (MTP), businesses can elevate their vision and mission to actively contribute to these global goals.

Massive Transformative Purpose (MTP)

In a world of rapid technological advancements and disruptive innovations, businesses have the opportunity to think beyond incremental improvements and embrace a Massive Transformation Purpose–a bold, ambitious vision that inspires change.

Coined by Singularity University, an MTP challenges companies to think exponentially, to dream big and envision what could be possible if there were no limitations. It is not just a mission statement, it is a guiding principle that fuels innovation and drives societal impact.

A strong MTP is:
- **bold and audacious**: challenging the status quo and daring to dream big
- **inspiring**: energising your team and stakeholders

- **purpose-driven**: focusing on meaningful change
- **open-ended**: encouraging continuous innovation and exploration

Examples of strong MTPs from SMEs:
- **Extremis** designs tables, chairs and benches, loungers, et cetera. Their MTP is: **"We create tools for togetherness"**.
- **Umbrosa** offers a collection of umbrellas and shade sails for both residential and commercial applications. Their MTP is: **"We create shadow"**.
- **XPRIZE foundation** by Peter Diamandis wants to **"Design and operate competitions to incentivise breakthroughs that benefit humanity"**.
- The MTP for a drone start-up could be **"To revolutionise disaster response and save lives"**.

These statements do more than simply describe what these companies do: they set the stage for innovation, unlock new opportunities, and align their efforts with a higher purpose. With an MTP in place, businesses focus on exploring transformative solutions rather than settling for incremental change.

To reach your destination–whether it is your vision, mission, or MTP–you will need effective navigation through:
- **course management**: staying on track requires clear processes for monitoring progress on strategic goals. This includes regular performance reviews, key metrics tracking, and structured decision-making frameworks.
- **course correction**: while consistency is key, businesses must also have processes in place to adjust strategy when external conditions shift. This means, e.g., scenario planning, real-time data analysis, and iterative decision-making to allow for recalibration without losing sight of your strategic goals.
- **risk management**: identifying, assessing and mitigating risks before they become major obstacles.

2.3 Ecosystem

Building a strong speedboat business is not just about assembling the right crew and constructing a high-performance vessel. No matter how powerful your engine or how effective your navigation system, external forces shape your journey.

A boat never sails in isolation–it moves within a dynamic ecosystem that influences its speed, direction, and success. By understanding and engaging with this broader environment, you can seize opportunities, mitigate risks, and build long-term resilience.

We will explore three fundamental aspects of this ecosystem:
- the **weather**: symbolising external forces such as market conditions, emerging trends, and disruptions that can shift overnight, from clear skies to sudden storms
- the **ocean**: representing the foundation on which your boat sails. While calm waters may seem ideal, agile speedboats must be ready for rough waters and alert to early ripples.
- the **swarm**: a mix of neighbouring vessels–e.g., drones, fishing boats, container ships–that can pose challenges but also offer opportunities for collaboration

Weather

The first factor shaping your ecosystem is the weather. Sometimes, you sail under clear skies with favourable winds, while at other times, sudden storms test your resilience. In business, the weather represents market dynamics, economic shifts, and external forces that can either support or challenge your growth. To navigate these changing conditions, you need a dedicated follow-up system–much like a weather forecast. This helps predict shifts in the business environment and assess their speed.

One such forecasting system that is often applied within speedboat businesses is trend watching. This involves actively tracking market trends, industry developments, and customer behaviour through, e.g., social media, industry reports, newsletters, and networking. Additionally, market research helps detect shifts early on, while regular customer analysis helps verify whether their needs and expectations are still in line with your offering.

Next to classical forecasting methods, which use facts that are at hand, foresight challenges you to look beyond the horizon and identify emerging technologies, business methods and models that help imagine and create the future instead of just trying to predict it.

Foresight methodology: navigating uncertainty with scenario planning
Prediction vs foresight

In innovation, foresight methodology helps businesses anticipate disruptions by developing scenario planning–a structured approach to navigating uncertainty. Unlike traditional forecasting, which extends known trends to predict a single future, foresight maps out multiple possible futures, preparing businesses for a range of potential outcomes.

The key difference lies in how uncertainty is handled:
-   **Prediction** (forecast planning): focuses on a single expected future, assuming stable trends and gradual changes. Businesses that rely solely on prediction risk being blindsided by sudden disruptions.
-   **Foresight** (scenario planning): identifies uncertainties and unknowns, exploring different ways the future could unfold. By considering multiple scenarios, businesses can develop proactive strategies for various possibilities, turning risks into opportunities.

By applying foresight, companies leverage past industry experiences to anticipate potential shifts and prepare response strategies–using their speedboat's agility to steer clear of risks or capitalise on emerging trends.

Understanding uncertainty with PESTEL analysis

To better understand external uncertainties and unknowns, a **PESTEL** analysis provides a structured framework for assessing macro-environmental factors. It helps identify key Political, Economic, Societal, Technological, Environmental, and Legal factors that may impact your business:

- **Political**: Government policies, trade agreements, political stability, et cetera can influence business operations.
- **Economic**: Inflation, interest rates, market fluctuations, et cetera can affect consumer behaviour and financial planning.
- **Societal**: Demographic shifts, cultural trends, changing customer preferences can reshape demand.
- **Technological**: Automation, emerging technologies and innovations may disrupt industries or create new opportunities.
- **Environmental**: Climate change, sustainability concerns, regulatory pressures et cetera can impact operations and corporate responsibilities.
- **Legal**: Compliance with regulations, labour laws, industry-specific legal requirements can require major adjustments in business processes.

Foresight builds on these PESTEL outcomes to anticipate risks and future trends and prepare adaptive strategies.

Neither forecasting nor foresight are enough, though. It is just as important to develop tools and scenarios that prepare your business for when a storm hits. Detecting a shift in the business environment only has value if you know how to respond. Should you adjust your direction? Slow down? Accelerate? Can you use the storm to your advantage?

If you wait until the weather changes or the storm hits before reacting, you risk being too late or making rushed decisions out of panic. However, with a solid forecasting system, you can anticipate changes and even turn them into opportunities. Preparation allows you to adjust your course with confidence instead of reacting in crisis mode. Consider tools such as:

- dedicated trend watching beyond your own market
- regular scenario planning exercises
- continuous learning and development
- a data structure that supports predictive analysis
- regular engagement with key stakeholders
- integrating foresight thinking into board-level governance

Ocean

The ocean represents the vast, unpredictable environment in which every business operates. Setting sail on open water requires courage, determination, and a willingness to embrace the unknown. Once you leave the safety of the harbour, you cannot control the ocean–you can only learn to navigate it, adapt to its challenges, and chart a course towards your destination.

Starting a business follows the same principle. The biggest hurdle is often the first "yes": the decision to take the leap into entrepreneurship. Many never make that jump, held back by fear of the unknown, waiting for someone else to validate their idea. But once past that hurdle, the real journey begins. The ocean will not always be calm, but with maturity, expertise, and perseverance, you can overcome obstacles as long as you stay committed to your destination.

For start-ups and scale-ups, the first stage often feels like navigating uncharted waters. In these moments, focusing on the horizon–your vision and long-term goals–is essential. As discussed earlier, having a clear direction and effective navigation system prevents you from losing orientation, even in unfamiliar waters.

Then there are the waves that define your journey. Instead of avoiding them, learn how to ride them. Mastering the waves is like learning to surf:

- **First**, you focus on staying afloat, observing how your boat performs at sea. This means taking small, controlled steps: leaving the harbour for a first experiment, testing the waters with a focus group or customer interviews.
  Next, you sail a little further, catching the first ripples. This stage is about understanding how your product or service interacts with the market, and identifying potential obstacles before a full launch.
- **Once** you are sailing the open sea, rough waters are inevitable. While you cannot control the waves, you can learn to read them and anticipate changes. Even the smallest ripple can signal a major transformation ahead.

Navigate your business with Lean Startup

To read the subtle shifts in your business environment, the Lean Startup method by Ash Maurya offers a powerful approach. A key tool within this method is the Lean Canvas. This is a structured, one-page framework for analysing the critical elements to start or grow a business: problem, solution, customer segments, revenue streams, cost structure, et cetera.

Ideal for early-stage businesses, this tool helps test assumptions, spot dependencies, and refine strategies before major investments. Completing a Lean Canvas not only sharpens your business model but also strengthens your ability to anticipate challenges–like mastering small waves before sailing into deeper waters.

PROBLEMS	SOLUTION	UNIQUE VALUE PROPOSITION	UNFAIR ADVANTAGE	CUSTOMER SEGMENTS
	KEY METRICS		CHANNELS	
COST STRUCTURE		REVENU STREAM		

The better you understand the ocean and waves, the further you can venture from the shore and the richer your journey towards your destination. If you fear the waves too much, you will remain close to the harbour, limiting yourself to local markets and small-scale opportunities. But if you embrace the challenge, you can expand beyond borders, grow internationally, and even build new boats to accompany you on your journey or explore new destinations.

The deep ocean represents the unknown, which some see as a danger. But why not treat it as a resource, filled with potential, undiscovered opportunities? Entering a new market is like sailing into deep waters for the first time. It is unfamiliar, but rich with insights waiting to be explored. Understanding these depths can help you position your business. If you only sail on the surface, without being aware of what is happening underneath, you risk missing a strong foundation.

The ocean is more than just a powerful force to conquer, it also serves as a vast source of information. By observing the currents and other vessels around you, you can gather insights into where opportunities lie and how best to steer your boat towards them.

And finally, never forget that the ocean has tides, just like business. It moves in cycles, with ups and downs that must be managed wisely. The highs will fuel you with energy, giving you the strength to push forward. The lows, in turn, should be seen as valuable moments of preparation: time to reassess, adjust, and get ready for the next rise.

Swarm

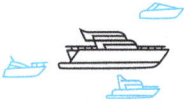

Surrounding every speedboat business is a swarm of other vessels–ranging from nimble start-ups and suppliers to container ships setting industry standards–all operating within the same ecosystem, all following their own course. While some pose competitive risks, others offer opportunities for collaboration through open innovation, corporate venturing, or joint value creation.

Success increasingly depends on identifying key players, recognising your own role within this broader swarm, and knowing when to steer alone and when to sail together.

Blue oceans vs red oceans

An influential concept on this topic comes from *Blue Ocean Strategy* by W. Chan Kim and Renée Mauborgne. They highlight the difference between red oceans–overcrowded oceans where multiple companies aggressively compete for the same market–and blue oceans, market spaces with fewer competitors, allowing greater freedom and differentiation.

The swarm effect

Sometimes, agility and resilience come from acting in unison–like a school of fish. A dynamic, decentralised, and adaptable swarm allows each participant to retain its identity and autonomy while coordinating efforts in respond to environmental changes. When each vessel contributes to a shared purpose, the entire fleet benefits from collective strength, ensuring that each boat not only survives but thrives in an ever-changing seascape.

Open innovation

Open innovation extends this idea of collaboration by involving external partners, such as customers, suppliers, or research institutions. This model fosters sharing ideas, knowledge, and resources to co-create solutions.

Key benefits of open innovation:
- **diverse perspectives**: tapping into a broader range of ideas boosts creativity and innovation potential
- **cost-efficiency**: pooling development efforts and sharing resources helps reduce R&D expenses
- **faster time-to-market**: leveraging external expertise accelerates development and shortens launch cycles
- **greater agility**: involving external partners enables quicker responses to market and technological changes
- **lower risk and barriers to entry**: sharing innovation responsibilities reduces individual risk and eases access to new opportunities
- **stronger collaboration**: engaging with external stakeholders builds trust and fosters deeper, cross-sector relationships
- **access to new markets**: partnering with diverse players opens doors to previously unreachable customer segments or regions
- **sustained competitive advantage**: continuously integrating fresh ideas helps maintain relevance in fast-evolving industries
- **enhanced problem-solving**: co-creating with others brings in novel approaches that lead to more effective solutions

While open innovation drives efficiency, cost-effectiveness, and innovation, it also entails shared ownership. In other words, your speedboat may no longer be entirely your own; you join other vessels in a broader, collaborative journey.

If you want to learn more about how open innovation can impact your IP strategy and business, be sure to read the section on Swarm in Chapter 3.

Corporate venturing

As a start-up speedboat, you may attract the attention of a large corporate–a "container ship"–looking to invest or collaborate. These large companies, with their solid business models and structured processes, often struggle with agility. Partnering with a nimble start-up like yours allows them to navigate change more effectively–while giving you the scale and support to accelerate your journey.

Key benefits of corporate venturing for speedboat businesses:
- **access to funding**: Corporate investments provide financial resources to support product development, scaling, and talent acquisition.
- **credibility boost**: Association with a well-known corporate partner enhances trust with customers, investors, and other stakeholders.

- **industry expertise and mentorship**: Start-ups benefit from the experience, insights, and strategic guidance of seasoned corporate professionals.
- **market access and distribution**: Corporates can open doors to established sales channels, customer bases, and global market.
- **technical resources and infrastructure**: Access to tools, facilities, or platforms that may otherwise be unaffordable or inaccessible for early-stage ventures.
- **faster validation and learning**: Collaborating with corporates enables quicker testing, feedback, and refinement of products or services.
- **stronger IP position**: Working with a corporate partner may include support in developing or protecting intellectual property.
- **increased visibility**: Corporate backing can generate media attention and attract interest from other investors or partners.
- **potential exit or acquisition pathway**: A venturing relationship can lead to a future acquisition or long-term strategic partnership.

If you want to understand how you can engage in a corporate venturing journey while securing your business growth, explore the tips in the section on Swarm in Chapter 3.

Wrapping up

In this chapter on building your speedboat, you have explored the key elements needed to create a business that is ready to be secured.

Next, Chapter 3 will focus on the safety measures–both critical and highly recommended–to secure your business and ensure it can grow safely over the next five years and beyond.

Chapter 3
Secure your speedboat business

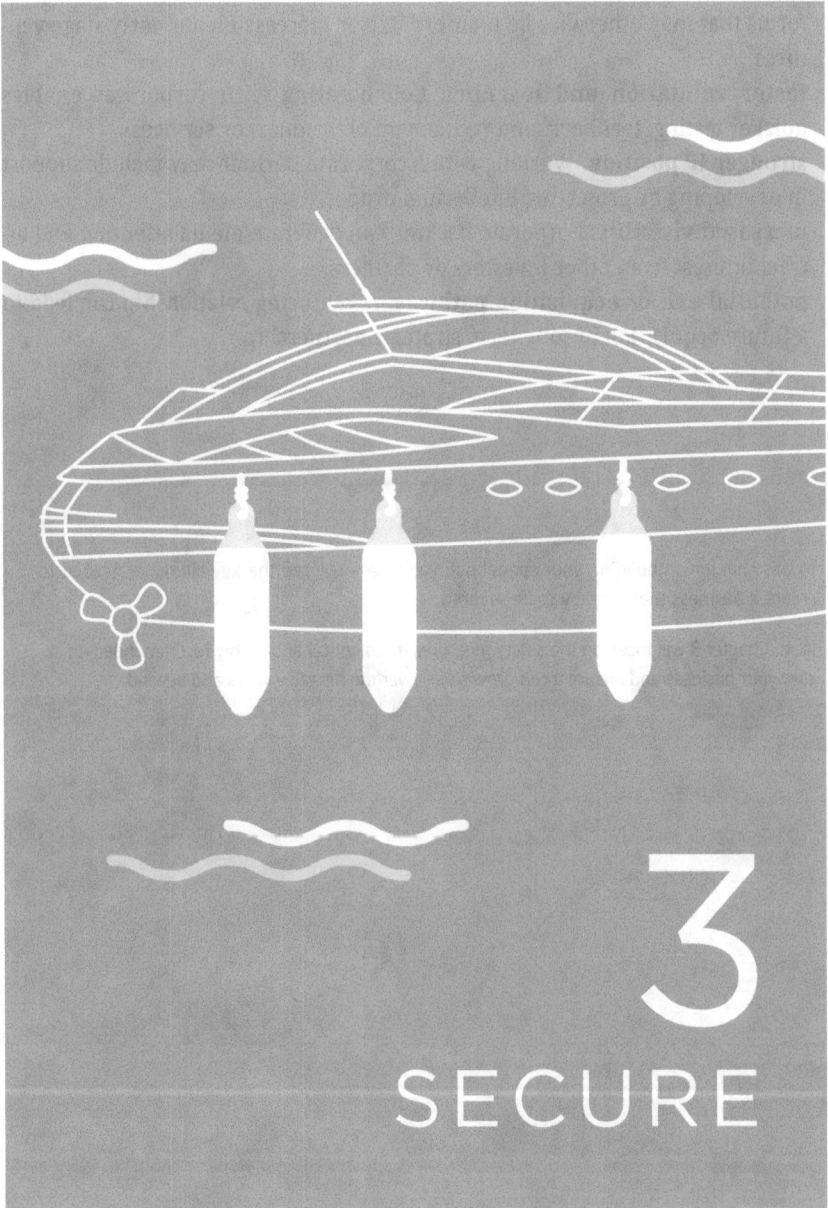

https://doi.org/10.1515/9783111673547-003

3.0 Introduction

> **What to expect**
>
> In the next chapter, you will discover how to take the right measures to ensure your boat remains safe, agile, and future-ready over the next five years.

You have designed your speedboat–a business built for agility, innovation and growth. But a well-built vessel alone is not enough. To navigate the open waters of your market with confidence, you need to secure it against risks that could slow you down or throw you off course.

This is where intellectual property comes in–not as a bureaucratic hurdle or a legal afterthought, but as a strategic tool that keeps your business ahead. Securing your business is not just about protecting it from threats; it is about ensuring continuity, creating a foundation for scaling, and building long-term sustainability.

Before exploring in detail how to secure your business per core aspect of your speedboat business–people, construction, and ecosystem–here are some key guidelines that will help you lay the groundwork for a strong and adaptable IP strategy.

Securing vs protecting

When launching a business, the last thing you want are fences around your product or service that limit growth, lock in development, or block shifts in your business model. You want to set sail freely, without being held back by competitors or constrained by third-party IPR.

That is why IP should not be about **protecting** your business, but about **securing** its freedom to grow and evolve. The difference is more than just semantics–it is a shift in mindset.

Taking a security-approach ensures your boat is safe when it is launched at sea. You take all necessary precautions to prevent others from infringing on your rights. You secure the most crucial parts of your business so you can make quick moves without disrupting your entire IP framework. In this way you gain freedom instead of restrictions.

A few things to keep in mind to achieve a successful security-approach:

- **Align IP with your business model**, not the other way round. Secure the most critical elements that allow your company to pivot and scale, rather than over-defining every possible feature to prepare for litigation.
- **Focus on business continuity**. Secure your core technology, brand, and competitive advantage to ensure your company remains resilient through changes and challenges.
- **Don't forget to think ahead.** Consider how your business may evolve in the next five years. Will your current IP choices still make sense if you expand into new products, markets, or sectors?
- **Use IP to generate revenue**. Consider licensing models, partnerships, and collaborations that allow you to expand your market reach instead of solely focusing on legal defence.

Your IP strategy should be a growth tool, not a defensive mechanism. Once you understand your scalability, you can integrate it into your IP strategy and choose registrations that are adaptable to different business models, allowing you to maintain market focus while opening opportunities for licensing and expansion in other areas.

IP management vs IP strategy

As mentioned in Chapter 1, IP management refers to the operational handling of registrations and (internal) procedures, while IP strategy involves the strategic choices made to reach the goal or final destination of your speedboat. Understanding the difference between IP management and IP strategy is essential, as the two are often confused–yet, each plays a distinct and critical role in building a resilient, future-proof business.

This chapter covers IP management through the lenses of people, construction, and ecosystem, while IP strategy is addressed in the section on the navigation system.

IP investment vs Return On Investment

Securing your IP is key, but it does come with a price tag. Some types of IPR, such as trademarks and design protection, are relatively affordable. Patents, however, can be costly, with upfront expenses often exceeding €10,000. Thus, investing in IP should be based on Return On Investment (ROI), not just legal necessity.

Many companies carefully calculate the ROI for product or service development–apply the same logic to IP, viewing IP investments as an integral part of your development budget.

		LOCATION	APPLICATION COST	TIMING
IP RIGHTS	TRADEMARK	NATIONAL	€ 1,000	Duration 10 Years
		EUROPE	€ 2,000	Duration 10 Years
	DESIGN	NATIONAL	€ 1,000	Duration 5 Years
		EUROPE	€ 2,000	Duration 5 Years
	PATENT	NATIONAL	€ 10,000	With the Application
		EUROPE	€ 40,000	For the First 4-5 Years
		UNITED STATES OR OTHER	€ 30,000	For the First 4 Years
LITIGATION	PATENTS	EUROPE	€ 8,00,000	5 Years
		BELGIUM	€ 2,00,000	10 Years
		US	€ 30,00,000	5 Years

Avoiding **infringement** and ensuring Freedom To Operate (FTO) is crucial, especially when managing your IP budget. Even unintentional infringement can lead to costly litigation, with expenses often exceeding what you would have invested in your own IP rights. In many cases, such legal battles can lead to bankruptcy or bring your journey to an abrupt end.

That is why analysing the IP strategies within your ecosystem is essential to protect your speedboat from legal threats and keep it sailing forward.

Doing it alone versus return on Investment

As a small business, your IP resources are not limitless. But that does not mean you must handle everything yourself. Knowing when to seek guidance is as important as understanding what you can do on your own.

what can you do yourself

- **Foster** an IP-aware culture within your company.
- **Keep track** of your IP measures and stay alert to new opportunities.
- **Monitor** industry developments and competitors.
- **Identify** potential IP risks early.

when best to seek guidance

- **Registrations:** IP offices can guide you through the process.
- **Contracts**: Even for standard templates, consult an IP lawyer to avoid costly misunderstandings.
- **IP strategy**: Work with an IP strategist who understands both the legal landscape and your business to align your IPR with long-term goals.
- **Commercialisation**: Involve a licensing manager to negotiate and manage licensing deals while securing fair compensation.
- **Enforcement**: Appoint an IP lawyer experienced with cease-and-desist notices and customs procedures to combat counterfeiting.
- **Valuation and tax**: Seek an accountant familiar with IP valuation and related tax incentives.

Securing your business is not about doing everything alone–it is about knowing where to focus your efforts and when to bring in expertise, so your business can grow with confidence.

Keeping these key guidelines in mind, we are now ready to dive into your speedboat business and find the best ways to secure all core aspects of your business, starting with the construction.

3.1 Construction

Here, unlike in Chapter 2, we begin by looking at how to secure the construction of the boat before turning to the people on board. This is because it is crucial to grasp the principles of IPR before anything else. These rights will later shape how you structure contracts with your crew and how you safeguard your journey within the broader ecosystem.

The construction elements of a speedboat can be secured through various IPR. These typically include:

- trademark: for the company name
- design registration: for the hull
- copyright: for drawings of the boat
- patent: for the engine
- know-how: for the fuel
- FTO: for the horizon (market/competitive space)

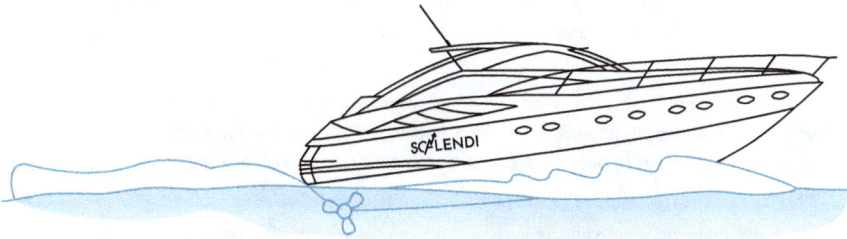

Key considerations

Before moving on to the details on how to secure the construction of your speedboat business, here are some key considerations to keep in mind when choosing the right IPR.

The impact of your business model

Before securing IPR, think beyond today: Consider how you will sell your product or service over the next five years. Your business model will shape your strategy and vice versa:

- **Selling** your speedboat? Your business model then focuses on offering one type of boat to a specific market.
- **Using** your speedboat as a tool to deliver your services? Your business model revolves around selling services, enabled by your speedboat.
- **Allowing** others to build on or use your speedboat? Your business model is licensing your product or service.
- **Expanding** to new horizons? If similar challenges exist elsewhere, then your business model is scaling through extra markets.

Many small companies avoid these questions in the early stages, but they are essential for scaling successfully.

Inventor or entrepreneur? Knowing what you really want

A flooring contractor developed a device to streamline the manual labour he performed every day. By taking all relevant factors into account, he created a highly efficient tool that not only saved him considerable time but also made the entire process simpler and more ergonomic.

He wanted to protect his invention and asked for advice on obtaining a patent. When asked about his motivation, however, it turned out he mainly wanted recognition for his idea rather than planning to become a product developer or establish a company to market his device.

If his sole intention was to ensure exclusive use, simply keeping the tool out of sight might do the trick, given that he typically used it only in enclosed spaces. Opting to patent would make the technical details publicly accessible, which could potentially inspire competitors to develop a similar tool.

Thus, before investing in a patent, at the very least he needed to explore partnerships with companies interested in commercialising his invention. Such collaborations could help offset the cost of filing the patent and potentially turn his innovation into a profitable venture.

Understanding the difference between the key components of your boat

IP measures should be strategic, not all-encompassing. Since resources are limited, focus on what truly drives your business growth. To do so, you need to understand the difference between the components of your boat, not just at the launch, but also when scaling your business.

When scaling, ask yourself whether your next solution will be a completely new boat design, or will only certain parts change?
–   If the entire product or service is new, patenting the whole boat makes sense.
–   If the core technology (e.g., the engine) remains the same–which is often the case–focus on securing the engine, rather than the boat or secondary aspects like the hull, which may change with different markets or customers.

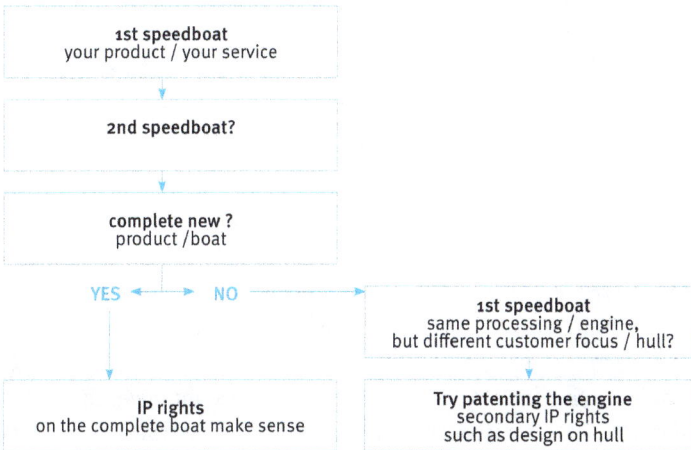

```
┌─────────────────────────────────┐
│        1st speedboat            │
│  your product / your service    │
└─────────────────────────────────┘
              │
              ▼
┌─────────────────────────────────┐
│        2nd speedboat?           │
└─────────────────────────────────┘
              │
              ▼
┌─────────────────────────────────┐
│        complete new ?           │
│         product /boat           │
└─────────────────────────────────┘

  YES ◄────► NO ──────────────►  ┌──────────────────────────────────┐
   │                             │        1st speedboat              │
   │                             │  same processing / engine,        │
   │                             │  but different customer focus / hull? │
   ▼                             └──────────────────────────────────┘
┌──────────────────────────┐                   │
│        IP rights         │                   ▼
│ on the complete boat     │     ┌──────────────────────────────────┐
│ make sense               │     │   Try patenting the engine        │
└──────────────────────────┘     │     secondary IP rights           │
                                  │   such as design on hull          │
                                  └──────────────────────────────────┘
```

Too often, start-ups file multiple patents to "protect as much as possible". However, a single, well-chosen patent can provide stronger business leverage. Before letting patent attorneys draft your patents, dig deeper into what truly drives your competitive advantage.

Patent smarter, not harder

One company developed a textile-based invention with applications across multiple markets. To protect against counterfeiting, they pursued at least three separate patents–one per market–based on minor differences in implementation.

Yet, at its core, the invention addressed a single problem with a single solution. Each patent merely adjusted the product description and claims to support infringement detection.

A smarter approach could have been a single, well-crafted patent centred on the core problem-solution, with market-specific variations included in the description. This would have offered similar protection, while reducing complexity.

By refining their patent strategy and focusing on the true innovation and scalable core, they could have saved time, money, and administrative burden without compromising protection.

The name of your speedboat

So far, we have talked about knowing the difference (in impact) between the key components of your boat, but we have not touched on its name. While the name of your company or product is not part of your boat's construction, it plays a crucial role–it sets the tone for your brand, shapes first impressions, and affects customer recall. So take your time in choosing and securing it properly.

Common naming mistakes to avoid

- **Being too descriptive**. New businesses often name themselves after what they do, but this rarely creates a strong brand. Instead, pick a name that conveys emotion or uniqueness, like Zumba, which suggests energy without explaining the product.
- **Skipping a trademark check**. A free domain name does not mean the trademark is available. Use tools such as TMview[2] to check for existing trademarks and avoid costly legal disputes.
- **Phonetic conflicts.** Trademark law considers how a name sounds, not just its spelling. If it sounds too similar to an existing brand, it may still be rejected.
- **Unintended meanings**. A name that works perfectly in one language may be problematic in another. Always check translations to prevent reputational risks.

The name of your boat should be unique, memorable, and strong enough to carry you forward. Choose wisely and secure it properly to ensure smooth sailing for your brand.

---

2 www.tmdn.org/tmview/#/tmview

Lost in translation: When a perfect brand name is not so perfect after all

A design company wanted to create a brand name for a new application. Since the concept needed to have a Scandinavian look and feel, they drew inspiration from words in their own language, altering them to sound more Scandinavian.

They quickly believed they had found the perfect brand name, that is, until they ran it through a translation app to check its actual spoken meaning. It turned out to have a completely unintended and unsuitable meaning, which would have undermined the product's value.

It is always advisable to translate a brand name into the languages of your target markets to ensure it is interpreted correctly, especially for creative names.

Securing your name

We call a registered name a **trademark**. Take the following steps to secure your boat's name:

1. **Check domain name availability**. Before proceeding, ensure that the desired domain name is available to secure a consistent online presence.
2. **Search trademark databases**. Use freely accessible databases such as TMview to check whether the trademark is already registered or in use.
3. **Seek professional guidance.** Consider consulting a trademark expert to navigate the process effectively and avoid potential conflicts.
4. **Determine geographic coverage**. Define the relevant regions where you intend to use the trademark, planning for at least the next five years.
5. **Clarify purpose.** Identify the intended use of the trademark over the next five years, ensuring it aligns with your business strategy.
6. **Register before launch**. Ideally, register the trademark **before** publicly launching the brand name to secure your rights and prevent disputes.

In the EU, a trademark is valid for ten years and can be renewed indefinitely. The registration cost is typically under €2,000.

Hull

The design of your hull (see also Chapter 2) is tailored to your customers and target market. A distinctive shape helps your product or service stand out, making it valuable to protect.

Ways to secure the hull

There are several ways to protect the outward appearance of your solution.
- **Copyright.** This is the easiest and most straightforward way. Automatically granted upon creation, copyright protects any creative work, including drawing and designs. While no registration is required, it is crucial to document the date of creation and clearly state copyright ownership.
  Copyright suffices for written documents, marketing materials, drawings, artistic works, et cetera.

- **Unregistered design (for EU)**. This is a rather "soft" method to secure designs for a short period of time. No registration is needed in Europe, but you must make your design public and document date of publication (and creation). Unregistered design is typically used for short-lived, seasonal, or hype-driven products within EU markets.

- **Registered design (EU) or design patent (US)**. This is the strongest form of design protection, requiring official registration. Some jurisdictions, such as the US, assess **novelty** and **non-obviousness** before granting protection. Registered design or design patents are the best option for physical products with a lifespan longer than three years and that will be repeatedly produced. Keep in mind though, that a registered design does not protect technical innovations or functional aspects of a product–only its appearance.

Tip

Design infringement is assessed based on customer confusion. If a competitor's product is visually similar to your product and thus could mislead customers, it may be considered infringement. In litigation cases, courts examine whether a company has exploited the success of a competitor by launching a lookalike product.

And the winner is ... not you: the award nobody wants

When teaching IP strategy, I often refer to Plagiarius,[3] a well-known German initiative that "rewards" the most shameless counterfeits with an ironic prize no company wants to win. Each year, they publicly expose companies that have blatantly copied original products, often displaying the counterfeit side-by-side with the genuine article.

The impact of this negative spotlight is real. In many cases, the publicity leads to swift action: counterfeiters are pressured into settling with the original creators, offering compensation or withdrawing the product altogether. For the original company, it becomes an unexpected yet effective form of enforcement, without ever stepping into a courtroom.

This is a brilliant and powerful reminder of why strong IP protection matters.

How to register a design?

1. Checking for availability on free accessible databases such as DESIGNview[4] is not an easy task; make sure your design is your own.
2. Seek for guidance.
3. Decide on geographic coverage with at least a scope of five years.
4. Decide on purpose or use with at least a scope of five years.
5. Register the design preferably prior to launching the name.

A registered design in EU is valid for five years and can be renewed indefinitely. Costs will be lower than €2,000.

Contract essentials

When working with external design companies or freelancers, secure your rights upfront.
- **Transfer of ownership**: Ensure contracts specify that the design belongs to your company.
- **Scope of use**: Clearly define how and where the design can be used, including potential future applications.
- **Prevention of disputes**: Avoid post-design discussions; ownership should be established before work begins.

---

3 www.plagiarius.com
4 https://www.tmdn.org/tmdsview-web/#/dsview

- **Third-party rights**. Confirm that the designer is not using copyrighted or licensed materials without proper permissions.

When licensing your product or service to others as part of your business model, you need–after, of course, securing your product or service–to draft a license agreement covering:
- **Scope:** Define where, how (long), and by whom the product can be (exclusively) sold or used.
- **Royalties:** Establish a measurable and enforceable royalty structure.
- **Minimum sales/use:** Prevent the licensee from passive holding rights without using them. This is often overlooked, but it is one of the most important elements.

Think before you print: When copyright comes back around

A restaurant owner hired a photographer to shoot images of various dishes for the menu. After paying for the photos, the owner assumed they could be used freely and indefinitely.

However, when the images were enlarged and used as wall decorations, the photographer issued an additional invoice–arguing that this use went beyond the original agreement and required separate compensation.

This type of misunderstanding is far from unique. Businesses, for example, often commission local artists to create a sculpture for their entrance hall, only to face legal issues when attempting to reproduce the work for commercial purposes.

Lesson learned? Always clarify usage rights upfront. Not only today's needs, but with a five-year horizon in mind. A photo taken at a workshop, for example, might seem minor now, but could later become key content for your marketing or branding. Thinking ahead helps avoid disputes and unexpected costs as your business scales.

Avoid infringement risks yourself

With the rise of generative AI, infringement cases are increasing, from music apps cloning artists' voices to design tools using protected artwork. As a start-up, avoiding such risks is critical. A small check can save you from costly legal battles and reputational damage.
- **Do not copy or use random online designs**. Many images and designs are copyrighted.
- **Be cautious with AI-generated content**. Ensure that AI tools use legally obtained training data, with respect for the creators.

- **If your speedboat is an AI company,** ensure that the database powering your queries is built with full respect for third-party IPR.

Engine

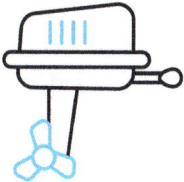

Why securing your engine?

Your business engine makes your product or service work. More than that, it is the powerhouse that drives your innovation and market success. Just like a finely tuned motor, it consists of multiple interlocking components–each solving a specific problem to keep your business moving forward.

However, without proper IP protection, even the most sophisticated engine can be vulnerable to competition, replication, or unforeseen legal roadblocks.

There are various ways to strategically secure your business engine:
- patents, for protecting technical inventions
- copyright, especially relevant when your engine is purely digital–as is often the case for SAAS companies
- a combination of patents and copyright, for digitally-driven engines

protecting the core of your engine through patents

Your business engine is a dynamic system–an intricate combination of problem-solving mechanisms that drive your product or service. Some solutions are straightforward, while others are innovative and unique to your industry or market.

Patents

A **patent** grants its owner the right to exclude others from making, using, or selling an invention for a limited time–typically 20 years–and within a defined geographical region. In return, the inventor must provide a detailed public disclosure of the invention.

To qualify for patent protection, an invention must meet the following key criteria:

- The invention solves a **technical problem**.
- **Novelty**: The invention must be new and not part of the existing state of the art.
- **First to file**: There is no prior patent application for the invention.
- **Inventive step**: The solution must not be obvious to a person skilled in the art; instead, it should offer an element of surprise or ingenuity.
- **Industrial applicability**: The invention must be tangible and applicable in an industrial context.

The concepts of novelty and first to file are often confused, but they refer to two distinct aspects of patent law. **Novelty** is about the invention itself–it must be new and not publicly disclosed before the patent application is filed. In contrast, **first to file** relates to timing: The right to a patent goes to whoever files the application first, regardless of who invented it first. Understanding this distinction is crucial: Even if your invention is novel, you could still lose the patent if someone else files it before you.

Before drafting patent claims, start by deeply understanding the problem-solution approach within your product or service. A well-defined problem-solution tandem is key–not just for patent protection, but for aligning with your current and future business models.

One common pitfall for start-ups is filing patents purely for defensive purposes–describing their technology in a way that prevents direct copying but does not strategically align with growth. Instead, focus on patents that safeguard the most scalable and commercially viable aspects of your engine:

- **Protective patents** primarily prevent competitors from direct replication but may lack focus on market expansion.
- **Scalable patents** target the core problem-solution combinations that will remain relevant as you grow and diversify.

Patent strategy: thinking beyond your first product

Let us compare the patent focus of two start-ups: ONAK, which produces foldable canoes, and Cheval Fatal, which has developed a drinking trough for horses. At first glance, they are quite similar companies, both innovating within niche markets.

ONAK's breakthrough innovation was finding a way to repeatedly fold and unfold plastic without causing creep and fatigue, making their canoe both portable and functional. Meanwhile, Cheval Fatal's innovation lay in integrating a photocatalyst into a concrete drinking trough to continuously disinfect water.

Both companies filed for patents, but their approaches differed:
–   ONAK patented pliable plastic with canoe applications mentioned in the description (US10266231).
–   Cheval Fatal patented a horse drinking trough that incorporates a photocatalyst element (BE201000475).

From a scalability perspective, the difference is striking. ONAK's patent protects a material innovation that could be applied far beyond canoes–potentially in other foldable, waterproof plastic products. In contrast, Cheval Fatal's patent is limited to a specific application, making it harder to extend into new markets.

So, when developing your patent strategy, ask yourself: Will you take the ONAK approach and patent a broader innovation with wide market potential, or follow the Cheval Fatal model and protect only one specific product?

Software and AI in patents

Many believe that software is not patentable. In reality, software *is* patentable as long as it addresses a technical problem in a novel, non-obvious way. The challenge is often that software developers jump straight to the solution and overlook clearly defining the underlying problem. Framing your software or AI-based invention around a technical problem-solution statement helps identify what aspects are truly patentable.

Think software cannot be patented? Think again.

A software start-up in the healthcare sector had developed detection software for a specific medical application. Initially, the team assumed that, because it was software, their invention could not be patented.

However, after taking a closer look at the essence of their innovation, they identified a clear technical problem their solution addressed. The algorithm at the heart of their solution–used to determine the accuracy of detection–met the key criteria for patentability, since patents are intended to protect solutions to technical problems.

Fortunately, they had not launched their invention or publicly disclosed their algorithm, allowing them to file a last-minute patent application. The patent was later granted in Europe, giving them a strong competitive advantage and significantly strengthening their position with investors. Recognising the opportunity for patent protection just in time, proved to be a crucial step in their growth journey.

Tip

AI-generated solutions face a unique challenge in patenting as patent law requires a human inventor, not an artificial one. Many AI start-ups assume this means patents are off-limits for their business.

Think again. Treat AI like a next-generation calculator, capable of processing vast amounts of data. You define the instructions, set the boundaries, and craft the search strategy–essentially creating a flow chart that guides AI in solving a problem.

These boundaries, strategies, and search methodologies can form the foundation of patent claims, preventing others from using the same approach to achieve similar results. In many cases, AI itself is not the invention, it is simply the tool executing a process you designed. And that process? Highly patentable.

Engine components: a hidden IP risk

The efficiency-enhancing solutions, or engine components so to speak, have no direct impact on your turnover. So when you are on a tight budget, the obvious choice would be to focus on patenting your core solutions instead of your engine components. However, these secondary solutions may be patentable too and could later be claimed by larger companies. If this happens, you risk being blocked from scaling your own technology.

One way to mitigate this risk is through defensive publication: publicly disclosing your secondary problem-solution approach and its connection to your product as a whole.

By making this information part of the state of the art, you prevent others from patenting it, as they will fail the novelty requirement. In essence, going public can be a strategic move to safeguard innovation while keeping it accessible.

Defensive publication: an often overlooked but effective strategy
What is defensive publication?

A defensive publication is a strategy to prevent others from patenting an invention by publicly disclosing it in detail. Once published, it becomes prior art, making it impossible for anyone else to claim a patent on that invention. Unlike patenting, a defensive publication does not grant the inventor exclusive rights, but it does safeguard the idea from being patented by competitors.

Why use defensive publication?
– **Cost-effectiveness**. It is generally cheaper than filing and maintaining a patent, particularly for inventions not central to your business model.
– **Freedom to operate.** By placing your invention in the public domain, you deny competitors the chance to lock it behind a patent.
– **Open contribution.** Defensive publications can foster innovation in your industry by sharing knowledge more broadly.

Key considerations
– **Market potential**. For inventions with limited commercial value to your business, defensive publication can be a practical alternative to formal patenting.
– **Level of control**. Opting for defensive publication means relinquishing exclusive rights, so consider whether you need ownership or if open access will do.
– **Quality of disclosure.** To be effective, the invention must be disclosed clearly and comprehensively, much like a patent application. Vague or incomplete descriptions may leave gaps for competitors to file patents on specific details.

Defensive publication is a powerful way to protect your innovation without the expense or commitment of patenting. By carefully choosing where and how to publish, providing thorough detail, and ensuring rapid disclosure, you can prevent others from monopolising your invention–while also contributing to a more open and collaborative environment for future innovations.

The hidden risk of keeping innovations secret

A SaaS company developed an application to detect visible safety hazards. Their software provided a technical solution that was eligible for patent protection, which they successfully secured.

The company had also invested significant time and effort into optimising detection algorithms and control subsystems to enhance speed and efficiency in detecting. However, since these components were not central to their business model, they decided–due to budget constraints–not to patent these engine subparts.

Some time later, they faced an unexpected challenge: A major industry player filed a patent that, while not covering their core software, restricted their ability to use these subsystems in future implementations. Because the start-up had never publicly disclosed these modules, they could not use prior art to challenge the patent.

Thanks to a good relationship with the larger company, no immediate problems arose. But the experience highlighted how easily the situation could have gone the other way. To avoid similar risks, they now consider publicly disclosing certain innovations to block others from patenting them later on.

How to apply for a patent?

Timing your patent application correctly is critical. Filing too early risks limiting your protection, while waiting too long could expose your invention to the public.

Practical tips:
– Identify the scalable problem-solution fit and assess its business value in relation to your business growth.
– Seek for guidance by a patent lawyer or patent attorney.
– Once your problem-solution (or combination of interdependent problem-solutions) is clear, you can start the application process.
– Before you do, conduct a patentability study to identify prior art patents. As an inventor, you may be convinced that you have come up with a totally new solution, but in reality, there are most likely already several similar solutions in place.
– Build your application on these prior art patents and describe in detail the innovative steps you took to end up with your unique solution. This will make your application stronger, withstanding thorough examination.
– Use your patentability study not only to strengthen your patent, but also to gain strategic insights into existing gaps in the market. This way, the cost of the study is quickly recovered.

Why you need a patentability study

A **patentability study (or search)** helps you assess if your invention qualifies for obtaining a patent. It checks the novelty, inventive step (or non-obviousness), and industrial applicability–the key criteria for patent approval.

The main goals are to:
– **Assess novelty**: Determine whether your invention is truly new and has not yet been publicly disclosed in existing patents, publications or any other sources of information.
– **Evaluate non-obviousness**: Analyse whether your invention involves an inventive step, or if it would be seen as an obvious improvement–or a logical next step–by someone skilled in the relevant field, based on existing knowledge and solutions.
– **Check industrial applicability**: Confirm that your invention can be applied in a real-world industry.
– **Identify prior art**: Identify any existing patents, publications or other publicly available materials that may be relevant to your invention. This also helps in assessing whether your invention meets the novelty and inventive step requirements.
A patentability study typically includes:
– **Patent search**: a thorough search of existing patents and patent applications, scientific journals, and other sources of prior art

- **Analysis of results**: a review of the prior art to see if the invention sufficiently stands out over what is already known
- **Patentability opinion**: a report that outlines whether your invention is likely to be granted a patent

As a patentability study can uncover potential roadblocks early on, it helps inventors and businesses save time and money before filing a patent application.

Copryright: another option to secure your digital enabled engines

For many start-ups, scale-ups, and SMEs–particularly those operating as SaaS companies–software is the engine driving their business.

While software is automatically protected by copyright, this protection only applies to the source code that makes the service run. It does not cover the underlying functionality or the service delivered. This means competitors can write their own code to achieve the same result without infringing on your rights.

Hence, if your software solves a technical problem, seeking patent protection may be a valuable option. There is also a third option for securing your engine: a hybrid approach where copyright secures the source code, while a patent secures the solution to the underlying technical problem. Use software flow charts to identify where specific technical challenges arose, and how you solved these.

Fuel

Know-how is the fuel powering your speedboat: the combined knowledge of all individual building blocks, how to turn them into high-performance systems, keep them running smoothly, and manage resources efficiently as your business scales.

Know-how thus includes practical knowledge, expertise or skills within a business, encompassing techniques, processes and experience that boost efficiency or foster innovation. Although it is not always confidential, well-managed know-how can significantly enhance the performance of both your engine and your speedboat (see Chapter 2).

For young companies, securing know-how is challenging. Much of it exists in people's minds, and limited resources often rule out investing in sophisticated knowledge management systems. As a result, these businesses must rely on internal procedures to document and protect this essential information.

Know-how also includes your data–an essential asset that should be carefully organised and stored in a structured database. This type of database is protected by database right, which is similar to copyright. It protects the structure of your data and prohibits third parties from downloading or extracting your data without permission.

By carefully safeguarding your know-how, you help ensure your speedboat continues to run smoothly and maintains its competitive advantage.

Fuel also becomes crucial when you are looking to sell your speedboat business. If, at that stage, the know-how exists only in the minds of your crew and has not been documented, you risk a lower valuation and a higher risk–will your crew stay on board if the speedboat gets a new captain? How this impacts your valuation will be explored in Chapter 4.

Fuel additives

Know-how includes all relevant knowledge, some of it hidden, some publicly available. Fuel additives on the other hand, are those extra elements that give you a competitive advantage. They are your unfair advantage (see Chapter 2): the pepper and salt of your know-how. They are never public and therefore treated as confidential information or trade secrets.

Securing trade secrets is not an easy feat. You must first identify which elements of your know-how are truly proprietary and repeat this assessment regularly. Once trade secrets are designated, you need robust measures to prevent leaks of these valuable insights, such as:
- restricting company visits
- providing clear guidance to your crew
- enforcing strict communication guidelines
- limiting data access to authorised personnel

Trade secrets are confidential pieces of information that provide a competitive advantage. They must have economic value and remain undisclosed to the public.

The crucial part of securing your business, is recognising whether you–as the captain–or someone in your crew holds an unfair advantage. Just as important is understanding how this advantage positions your business compared to your competitors.

Knowing your unfair advantage as an inventor, whether you are a founder or part of the team, means understanding why only *you* were able to develop a specific solution–one that would not be obvious to others. This can offer valuable insight into whether your innovation meets the inventive step requirement in patent law. After all, a solution based on an unfair advantage is unlikely to be obvious to someone skilled in the art. It is more likely to evoke the reaction: "Damn, why didn't I think of that?"

More than a hobby: turning dive experience into business innovation

A business manager with a background in precision mechanics and a passionate diver in his spare time, saw an opportunity where others did not. Drawing on his technical expertise and hands-on diving experience, he realised that the rebreather he used underwater could be made far more efficient. This insight led to the creation of a new company dedicated to developing high-performance rebreathers.

What made these rebreathers truly unique was the blend of professional know-how and real-world user experience. A textbook example of an unfair advantage–not something gained by luck, but earned through a rare mix of skill and passion.

Navigation system

In a speedboat business, your navigation system represents the strategic decisions that steer your venture–where to go, how to grow, and how to keep moving forward. With the different construction elements of your speedboat, you should be able to distinguish the different IPR possibilities and should be able to define your strategic know-how and trade secrets.

A holistic approach to IP vs focusing solely on IP rights

IP serves as a cornerstone of innovation, creativity, business strategy, organisational culture, and even ethics, influencing how ideas are valued, shared, and protected. In this way, the impact of IP rights reaches beyond ownership or control of ideas, shaping economic, social, and technological progress across industries and societies.

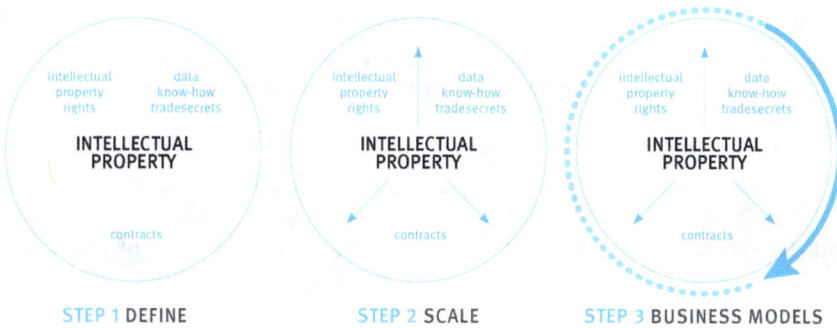

STEP 1 DEFINE   STEP 2 SCALE   STEP 3 BUSINESS MODELS

There is no need to overcomplicate things, but a structured approach–or at least a workflow–ensures you have the right measures in place *before* launching, reducing risks and giving you the freedom to scale confidently.

Navigating your IP: a three-step approach

Step 1: Map your current IP landscape
Start by taking stock of all your intellectual property.
- What can be secured through IPR?
- What contracts are already in place, and which ones will become relevant in the near future?
- What know-how exists within your crew, and what should be classified as a trade secret?
- What data is critical to your business?

Step 2: Look five years ahead
Next, take a forward-looking approach and consider how your IP might evolve.
- Will ongoing developments impact your IPR?
- Are existing contracts aligned with your future goals, or will they need to be updated?
- In which areas do you need to strengthen your know-how, and are you capturing trade secrets in time?
- Is your database structure strong and flexible enough to support future growth, or does it need adapting?

Step 3: Align IP decisions with your current and future business models
Finally, review your IP decisions in the context of both current and future business models.
- How are you selling your products or services today, and how might that change in the future?

These three steps help you manage your IP in balance with scalable growth.

You can apply this same three-step approach whenever you are filing for an IPR:
- trademarks: If your branding is likely to evolve within a year, consider registering a wordmark rather than a logo.
- patents: Think back to the ONAK vs Cheval Fatal case from the engine section.

Your IP is an asset, not just a legal formality. Treat it as a key part of your business strategy.

IP strategy: your navigation compass

For young or small businesses, an IP strategy is not about striving for an all-encompassing monopoly; it is about making targeted, cost-effective decisions that safeguard what matters most to your growth.

Key components of an effective IP strategy:
- **Prioritise the core innovations** that will have the greatest impact on your business.
- **Leverage cost-effective forms of IP**, such as trademarks, design rights, and utility models, where appropriate.
- **Protect trade secrets** through clear internal policies and robust confidentiality agreements.
- Take a **strategic approach to geographic coverage** by filing in the markets where you plan to operate.
- Consider starting with **national filings** in the first year, and explore **IP financing options** to spread costs over time.

By aligning your IP strategy with the way you navigate your speedboat business, you can secure key innovations, scale sustainably, and make the most out of a limited IP budget without overspending on protection. This approach helps you build strong, targeted protection while maximising long-term value as your company grows.

3.2 People

So far, we have focused on how to secure the construction of your speedboat, but that is only one part of the equation. Since navigating a speedboat involves people, it is equally important to take the necessary people-related measures to ensure your business can grow securely and sustainably.

We will explore the key roles of the captain, crew, and external support, outlining how each contributes to securing and scaling your business, and how you can protect your IP when collaborating with others.

Captain

As the captain, you are not just an IP owner. You are responsible for making IP decisions and following up on them, leveraging IP for business growth and sustainability.

The captain's IP roles

1. **Strategic IP decision-maker**

   Steering your company in the right direction also includes making strategic decisions about IP. You do not need to be an IP expert to do so, but you do need to grasp the essentials, understand what your IP is and how to leverage it. It is up to you to determine when and why specific IP protections-patents, trademarks, copyrights, or trade secrets-are necessary, ensuring they align with your business goals and market positioning. A well-crafted IP strategy is a powerful tool for securing competitive advantage, attracting investors, and driving long-term business continuity.

2. **IP coordinator and liaison**

   Though your IP professionals (e.g., patent attorneys, trademark lawyers) will handle formalities, it is up to you to understand their advice and translate it into business decisions. If needed, delegate this liaison role to an expert team member or work with an IP strategist to act as a translator between legal and business needs.

3. **Financial planner**

   IPR come with a cost. It is your responsibility to allocate funds, not just for the initial filing, but also for every step in the granting and post-granting process, including enforcement. Do not forget to continuously evaluate the cost-benefit of IP investments to ensure they contribute to business growth.

Bear in mind as well that IPR are territory-specific. Patents, e.g., define where a product or service cannot be built or sold. As global registrations can be very expensive over time, strategic geographical coverage is key:

- **Secure coverage** in areas where competition is strong and active.
- **Prioritise regions** where production is most likely.
- For Saas businesses, which automatically have a global market, a **Patent Cooperation Treaty (PCT) application** is often the best start. Once granted, there is time to refine your target countries.

4. **IP protector and enforcer**

   As captain of your speedboat business, monitoring and enforcing your IP rights are your responsibility–no one else will check for infringements. IPR come at a (considerable) cost, so if you are unwilling to act against infringement, reconsider whether the investment is worthwhile.

Does enforcement always mean going to court?

No, consider these steps to minimise the risk of third parties harming your business:
- **Step 1: Show you own IP**
  The first line of defence is making your ownership clear:
  - Use copyright symbols on leaflets, brochures, websites, et cetera. Copyright applies automatically to any original written or graphic creation without the need for registration or extra costs. So why not highlight it? It enhances professionalism and acts as a deterrent.
  - Use the ® or ™ symbol if your brand name is trademarked.
  - Clearly mark patent-protected products and marketing materials to reinforce your rights.

Displaying these signals demonstrates that you understand and take IP seriously. This may seem obvious, but it is often overlooked, despite requiring little investment.
- **Step 2: Take action when needed**
  Ignoring infringement sends the message that you will not defend your rights, inviting further violations. Instead:
  - Prepare a standard infringement letter (ideally with legal support). Most cases can be resolved through a simple letter or mediation. Having one ready gives you the confidence to act.
  - Assess legal action carefully if a letter does not do the trick:
    - Investigate the infringer's IP portfolio–are they repeat offenders?
    - Gather and timestamp evidence to strengthen your case.
    - Estimate potential business losses and weigh them against legal costs.
    - Consult IP lawyers on strategy and feasibility.
    - If proceeding, allocate a legal budget wisely.

---

5. **Knowledge guardian**

   As a captain, understanding and guarding the know-how of you and your crew is key. You need to distinguish between widely known industry knowledge and knowledge that is unique to your speedboat, your unfair advantage.

   Then ask yourself:
   - How valuable is this unique know-how?
   - What risks arise if a competitor gains access to it?

   If losing control of this information would harm your business, it must be protected as a trade secret–and, as the name implies, kept secret.

   This can be especially challenging for start-ups. As a newcomer to the market, you may feel pressure to prove your expertise, sometimes oversharing in an attempt to gain credibility. But revealing too much–even unintentionally–can jeopardise your competitive advantage.

   To safeguard your advantage:
   - Bear the purpose of meetings in mind. Share only what is necessary for the discussion.
   - Resist the urge to over-impress. More information does not always mean more credibility.
   - Be mindful of your surroundings. In public settings, you never know who might be listening.

6. **IP culture builder**

   As a captain of a speedboat business, one of your key responsibilities is to build an IP culture, both within your team and in interaction with third parties:

   - **Within your team**
     Encourage an IP-conscious work environment: Make sure your team understands the basics of IP and grows the reflex to report key discoveries before conducting public tests or discussing innovations with external parties. This allows you to put the necessary IP measures in place.

> **Tip**
>
> Assign IP-related tasks to key innovation team members, having them track industry patents and shifts in competitor IP strategies. Regular discussions–weekly or monthly–keep IP top of mind, reinforcing its strategic importance and integrating it into your company's innovation process.

- **With third parties**

  Build sustainable relationships with freelancers, subcontractors, and other third parties. Respect others' IP, demanding the same in return. Do not hesitate to discuss IP matters upfront–clarity prevents conflict.

> **Tip**
>
> Dealing with IP is an essential part of ethical business. If you are ever unsure about how to proceed, flip the scenario: Would you be comfortable if someone else did the same to you? If not, there is your answer.

Contract essentials: the founders' agreement

Unfortunately, friendships can quickly turn into conflicts when money is involved. So if there are multiple founders, a founders' agreement is essential. This is not just about signing a document–the discussions leading up to it are just as important. Starting this process early on, when the company has not even been formally established yet, will help you understand each founder's vision and commitment.

Key topics of a founders' agreement:
- share distribution and decision-making rights
- exit plans if a founder leaves
- strategies for continuity and growth

From mini company to major conflict

As part of a typical end-of-year project, four students launched a temporary *mini company*. What started as a school assignment quickly gained real momentum. Their business idea resonated, attracted attention, and even brought in early revenue. Encouraged by this unexpected success, they began discussing the possibility of continuing the venture after graduation.

But as the project evolved, so did the problems. The students had never clearly defined roles, responsibilities, and ownership. Differing visions and growing tensions around each student's contribution soon surfaced. Discussions turned into heated arguments. Eventually, the group fell apart: Two students carried on with the original concept, one walked away–frustrated by the lack of financial recognition–and the fourth started a competing business of his own.

What had begun with excitement and potential, ended in conflict and confusion. Much of this could have been avoided with a simple agreement upfront, outlining expectations, responsibilities, and what would happen if things did not go as planned.

Crew

The crew's roles

Your crew, both employees and freelancers, plays a vital role in both inventing and securing your business's intellectual property. A strong IP culture prevents accidental disclosures and ensures innovations can be leveraged.

Awareness and communication

Make sure your crew understands and follows your business IP strategy. It is equally important that they grow a reflex to communicate proactively about IP when they are developing new applications, products, or services. In this way, you can register IP at exactly the right time–neither too early nor too late.

Inventorship

An inventor is the person who created the product, process, or a part of it. Without a contractual transfer, an inventor may claim ownership of the invention. Since you have assembled your crew to help you innovate and stay ahead, inventorship is a key part of their contribution. It is important to note the legal distinction between inventions made by employees and those made by freelancers; the implications may vary per country. In Belgium, for example, inventions by employees typically belong to the company by default, while freelancers must explicitly transfer their rights. If your speedboat business files for a patent, you must ensure that all ownership rights are properly secured.

Even when crew members have no ownership, they do appreciate being listed as inventors, as it enhances their reputation, strengthens their CV, and reflects valuable contributions to innovation. This has no impact on ownership, but in this way, you officially acknowledge their contribution to the registered innovation.

Documentation and know-how protection

To safeguard continuity, capture your know-how in clear, structured processes. Skills may not always transfer, but well-documented methods do. Whether in software development, material innovation, or process improvements, make it a habit to record what you did-and why. A strong knowledge management system not only protects your intellectual assets but also makes your business more resilient and scalable.

Key tools
– Lab book: to record the time and date of new ideas, technical insights, and inventions. By documenting your independent development process, you can demonstrate when and how your ideas emerged.
– Regular registration of know-how and insights, including an official date stamp, such as:
    – the i-Depot system (Benelux trademark office)
    – registering documents at a notary or registration office
    – depositing copies of server back-ups with a notary

Mind you, such registration does not guarantee ownership or prevents others from patenting the same idea unless the information has been made public. Registration is, however, crucial to demonstrate prior art in case of disputes.

Tip

One of the biggest risks I see in businesses is that critical knowledge exists only in the minds of key individuals, never properly recorded. Time and again, I encounter companies where essential know-how is locked away, leaving operations vulnerable. If a key person leaves, falls ill, or faces unexpected circumstances, the entire business could stall. Documenting vital knowledge is not just about intellectual security, it is about survival.

Confidentiality management

Beyond documentation, it is crucial to control the information flow. Ensure your crew knows what can be shared and what must stay confidential. A well-informed team minimises the risk of accidental leaks.
– Limit full access to only a trusted few, while providing employees only the information necessary for their roles. The fewer people with the complete picture, the lower the chance of unintended exposure.
– External interactions also pose risks. A casual conversation at a networking event can reveal strategic insights, and employees inevitably retain the skills they learn. The key is not preventing knowledge transfer-it is managing

what is most critical. By proactively securing sensitive information, you safeguard your business, even as crew members come and go.

IP follow-up

Encourage your crew to help safeguarding your field by staying alert to new inventions, tools, and technologies. Make IP an integral part of the development process and treat IP measures as part of R&D investments rather than a separate expense.

Tip

To integrate IP into product development:
- Conduct regular FTO checks to avoid infringement risks.
- Use patent databases for inspirational searches and to monitor the competitive landscape.
- Encourage internal knowledge sharing to capture lessons learned and strengthen know-how.

- Align technical developments with the business strategy to identify and protect core IP.
- Schedule regular feedback sessions with your external IP expert to guide and adjust your approach.
- Conduct a thorough IP check-up before launching a new product. This is especially important if you are operating in a competitive IP landscape.

To integrate IP into R&D investments:
- Include the cost of IP protection measures as a standard part of your overall R&D budget.

Contract essentials

Payroll crew

When hiring payroll crew members, ensure their contracts include all necessary IP clauses.
- **Inventorship and ownership:** Clearly state that all inventions, copyrighted materials, or developed know-how automatically belong to the company.
- **Confidentiality:** Define rules that protect trade secrets and confidential information.
- **Non-compete:** Specify restrictions on working for competitors for a set period after leaving.

One more thing: Many employees pursue **side projects**. While they may assume their personal time is unrestricted, there is a major caveat: If an employee uses company expertise to develop competing or adjacent solutions, this could jeopardise your business. So make expectations clear from the outset. At the very least, require employees to seek approval before engaging in external business activities.

freelance crew

Freelancers work with your company on a structured basis but remain self-employed, meaning IP ownership does not transfer automatically. Their contracts require extra attention.

- **IP ownership:** Clearly stipulate that all work, inventions, and creations developed for your company are transferred to you. This must be in the contract from the start.
- **Confidentiality:** Trade secrets must remain protected, even after their contract ends.
- **Non-compete:** Freelancers cannot simply use or repurpose their work for another client upon leaving. A reasonable non-compete period should be agreed upon. Be mindful that overly strict clauses are likely to be contested, as these limit the freelancers' future opportunities.
- **Pre-existing IP risks**: Ensure freelancers confirm in writing that their work does not violate prior agreements or infringe on existing IP.

For start-ups and scale-ups, freelancers are often crucial in early stages when specialised expertise is needed. As the company grows, payroll staff often replace freelancers. However, the early stages are also when core IP is developed—making airtight contracts essential. Investors scrutinise IP structures, and unclear agreements can pose serious funding risks.

IT freelance crew

IT freelancers require extra attention when it comes to copyright, especially in coding. Unlike patents or trademarks, copyright by default belongs to the creator, not the company.

- **Payroll vs freelance**: Payroll employees automatically transfer copyright to their employer (though this should still be explicitly stated). Freelancers, however, retain ownership unless the contract specifies otherwise.
- **Full rights transfer**: Contracts must include a full transfer of economic and moral rights to any software developed for your company. Without this, freelancers could later claim ownership of core parts or demand additional payments for continued use.

- **Work-for-hire clause**: Clearly state that all code, algorithms, and technical developments created for your company belong to you from day one. This prevents disputes and secures your business.
- **Open source components**: Double-check the status of these components, including related clauses, in terms of security threats.

Support

Launching and growing a speedboat business often requires external support. However, these external parties are not bound by the rules that apply to your crew. Managing IP in such collaborations depends on the purpose of their involvement and their role:

Advisory purposes

When working with consultants, mentors, accountants, or suppliers for advisory purposes, you may need to share confidential details. In these cases, a **non-disclosure agreement** (NDA) or a **one-way contract** is essential.
- A one-way contract is appropriate when only your company is disclosing information, and the external party's insights do not influence your IP.
- Through an NDA the parties agree not to disclose any information covered by the agreement.

Even with an NDA in place, only share what is strictly necessary. Trust is not a safeguard, and a long-standing relationship is no substitute for a written agreement. While a **gentlemen's agreement** can work in informal settings, a formal contract helps prevent misunderstandings.

Does this mean you need an NDA for every conversation? Not necessarily. First, assess whether sharing confidential information is necessary to get valuable input. Many initial discussions can provide meaningful feedback without disclosing sensitive details. Learning how to communicate effectively while protecting your business is a crucial skill.

Contract essentials

There are situations where an NDA or a more formal contract is indispensable. If you collaborate with external designers, software developers, or other service providers, their contributions may directly shape your product or service. This makes it essential to establish clear agreements on IP and confidentiality.

An NDA is just the first step. Before engaging with external service providers, discuss IP ownership and transfer upfront. Do not proceed until key issues are clarified:
- **Transfer of ownership**
  If an external company contributes to your product or service, ensure that the IP becomes yours.
  - If a design company creates your boat's design, secure full ownership of both the design and copyright, or at least for the dedicated purpose.
  - If a software company develops code for your engine, ensure full copyright ownership.
  - If a supplier designs a mould for your product and suggests modifications, their input could impact the final product's IP. Ownership transfer should be agreed upon in advance.
- **Pre-existing IP**
  External providers may already own software copyrights, patents, et cetera. If their technology is integrated into your product, a **licence agreement** may be necessary. Such licences can coexist with IP transfer agreements, so clarifying this upfront is crucial.
- **IP warranty**
  Ensure that service providers own the IP they are using and that their work does not infringe third-party rights. Contracts should include an IP warranty clause, holding them liable for any infringement. This protects your business from future legal disputes.
- **Hold harmless**
  While an IP warranty ensures that service providers declare their work does not infringe third-party rights, a hold harmless clause goes a step further, requiring them to cover any legal costs, damages, or liabilities if infringement does occur. This provides an extra layer of protection and helps shield your business from financial risk.

After the initial discussions and NDA-backed conversations, a **collaboration agreement** must be in place before any actual work begins. This agreement should define:
– the purpose of the collaboration
– roles and responsibilities of both parties
– IP arrangements

> **Tip**
>
> A recurring issue is the distinguishment between **background knowledge** (i.e. existing expertise brought into the collaboration) and **foreground knowledge** (new knowledge developed together). Your agreement should cover foreground knowledge while allowing external parties to retain their background knowledge.

Small companies often overlook that universities or research centres bring extensive background knowledge and must retain its use for future research or collaborations, even with competitors. To prevent conflicts, the agreement should clearly state that while foreground knowledge from the project is transferred, the institution keeps the right to use its background knowledge. If background knowledge is needed to use the foreground knowledge, a licence is required to formalise its use.

When collaborating with universities, securing the right to apply for IPR based on foreground knowledge, is often possible. However, universities may also wish to **publish research findings**. While this might seem at odds with confidentiality, it can be managed by setting clear publication timelines, requiring prior approval, and asking for co-authorship.

Publication can even become part of your IP strategy. In some cases, publishing certain findings instead of patenting them ensures that your innovations enter the public domain, preventing competitors from securing exclusive rights over them. Additionally, having research from a respected institution support your technology strengthens your business's credibility and market position.

Why defining the purpose of collaboration matters

Defining the purpose of the collaboration in your agreement is essential for several reasons:
– **Clarity of intent**
    It explicitly states why the collaboration agreement exists and what both parties aim to achieve, ensuring everyone understands the objectives and scope from the start.

- **Guidance for interpretation**
  In case of disputes or ambiguities, the stated purpose provides context for interpreting specific clauses, helping to preserve the agreement's original intent.
- **Scope limitation**
  By clarifying the agreement's purpose, it limits obligations and prevents either party from straying beyond agreed objectives without renegotiating terms.
- **Legal enforceability**
  A well-defined purpose strengthens enforceability. Courts or arbitrators can refer to it when resolving issues or clarifying the agreement's intentions.
- **Alignment of expectations**
  It aligns both parties on the ultimate goal or outcome, reducing misunderstandings and ensuring the agreement fulfils its intended function.

Overall, a clearly defined purpose provides direction, minimises ambiguity, and helps the agreement serve its intended purpose.

Guidance on how to prepare for collaboration and structure your approach to a collaboration agreement can be found in the section on the swarm within your ecosystem, later in this chapter.

3.3 Ecosystem

Securing your business goes beyond people and products–it also requires a clear view of the ecosystem you are sailing in.

Your actions impact others, just as their actions influence you. You cannot sail blindfolded–securing your journey means staying aware of your surroundings, spotting both opportunities and threats as they arise. It is about making the most of what lies beneath your boat, while also using weather forecasts to steer wisely through changing conditions.

Weather

As a company you can prepare yourself for weather forecasts by different set-ups.

As we explained in Chapter 2, we should take advantage of the weather forecast to manoeuvre our speedboat and to adapt our plans according to what is coming.
We can do this through:

Trend watching

Securing your business via trend watching, means that you actively explore the patented technologies.

You can easily set up a query that gathers the most important problem-solution wording in your field, a query that assembles some insights on what is or could be going on in your sector. Not only does such a query give you insights on what is happening regarding the focused technology/problems/solutions, it also gives you an indication of the time line.

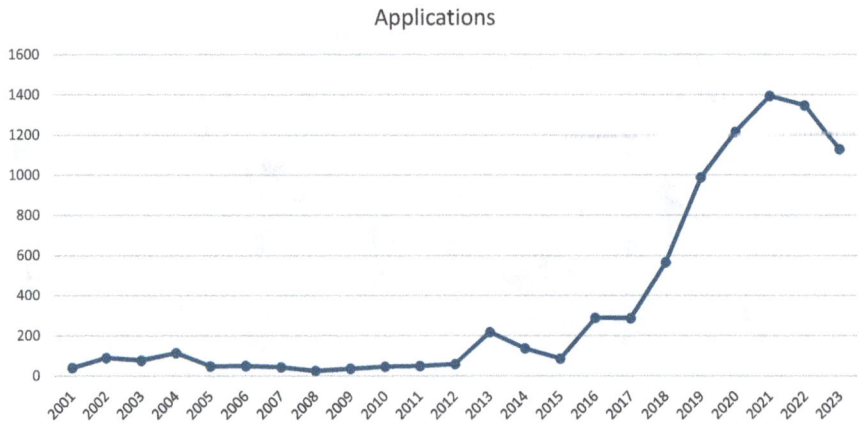

Applications

To illustrate this approach, an analysis was conducted using PATBASE, focusing on all patents containing a combination of the following keywords: (visi*) and (artificial intelligence) and (neur* and netw*). This query aimed to highlight the trend in patent filings where vision systems, artificial intelligence, and neural networks intersect.

The resulting graph reveals an initial ripple around 2013–an early indicator that change was on the horizon. From 2017 onwards, however, there has been a clear exponential increase in patent applications, suggesting a surge in focus and interest within this domain. This spike reflects breakthrough innovations or disruptive technologies gaining traction in the sector.

For entrepreneurs, 2013 would have been a signal to start paying attention, and by 2018, the opportunity to ride the wave was undeniable. Entering this field today presents greater challenges, and any new development should be preceded by a thorough FTO analysis.

Benchmarking

If you want to prepare a secured business, you need to analyse the IP strategy of your competitors and your sector.

Check whether your competitors have patents and whether they are still actively filing new applications. Do they own trademarks? Are they registering designs? Do they mention copyright in their website content or marketing materials? Much of this information can be found through free databases such as Espacenet,[5] Google Patents,[6] PatentStorm,[7] or national patent office websites. With just a short introduction or basic training, these tools can help you gather valuable insights into your competitors' IP strategies.

If some of your competitors are particularly active in filing IPR, it is wise to set up alerts that notify you of new applications or legal changes. This allows you to proactively secure your position and avoid possible infringement issues. Keep in mind, however, that it takes at least 18 months for a patent application to become publicly available. So remain especially cautious with (larger) companies that file aggressively. You can monitor this yourself by regularly repeating targeted

---

5 www.worldwide.espacenet.com
6 www.patents.google.com
7 www.patentstorm.us

searches, or by using (paid) databases that allow you to set up automated queries and receive regular alerts.

Forecasting

Just as analysing your competition is valuable, it can be equally insightful to examine your broader sector–specifically by tracking the number of patents being filed. One of the easiest ways to do this is by using patent classification codes. Through **Espacenet**, you can quickly identify the most relevant codes for your industry and monitor related patent activity:

By performing these searches regularly, you can stay up to date with developments in your field. You will start to notice when trends shift, and if something catches your attention, it is easy to dive deeper into the available information.

Ocean

Operating in a competitive environment means being prepared for potential IP disputes.

To avoid litigation:
- **Avoid infringement** to begin with.
- **Document your innovation process** to prove originality and differentiation from existing patents. This demonstrates that you not only have analysed patents thoroughly, but also that you have come up with a better solution.
- **Be mindful of marketing activities**. Make sure all relevant IP protections are in place before promoting a product or service. Require teams to request IP approval before launching any new campaign or introducing something to the market.

Freedom to operate

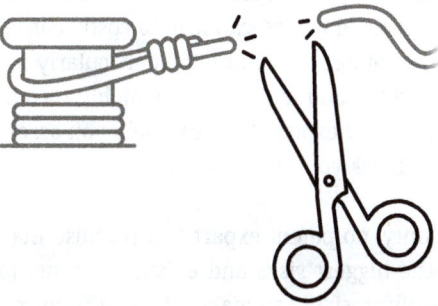

Before launching a product or service, you first need to ask yourself: Do I have the freedom to operate? In other words, are you legally allowed to bring your solution to market without infringing on someone else's IPR?

Too often, young companies assume that if they have not seen similar products or services, there is no problem to set sail. But in today's global, interconnected world, that is a risky assumption. Just because you have not come across a competitor, does not mean your path is clear, especially when it comes to IP.

That is why conducting an FTO analysis is essential. It helps you determine whether you are free to use, produce, or market your innovation without violating existing IPR. And it is not just about patents–it also includes trademarks, designs, copyright, and more.

There are several free or affordable tools to help you perform a quick cross-check:
- **For trademarks**, start with TMview (by the EUIPO).[8] You do not want to invest in branding, design a logo, and launch a marketing campaign, only to discover that your brand name is already taken. Changing a name after launch can be mentally and commercially painful.

> **Tip**
>
> When choosing a brand name, do not just check existing trademarks. Also translate it into common languages to avoid unintended meanings, and check domain name availability.

- **For designs**, use DESIGNview[9] and combine it with the correct Locarno classification to narrow your search. Design rights can be trickier to search, and while accidental overlap is less likely without (digital) contact between parties, it is still worth checking.
- **For patents**, use free databases such as Espacenet for an initial search. But be cautious: Patent infringement–intentional or not–can lead to costly consequences. A proper FTO study is hence not optional, but vital, particularly for tech companies. Because of the complexity and legal risk, it is highly recommended to consult a patent attorney or FTO expert. They can help you assess whether existing, active patents could block your business plans.

No FTO study can ever offer 100% certainty–no patent expert will promise that. But it *will* give you a clear picture of the biggest risks and existing patents to watch out for. And in business, that kind of foresight can make all the difference.

> **Tip**
>
> Don't confuse a FTO study with a patentability study, as they serve different purposes.
> - FTO focuses on risk, identifying active patents that could block your invention from market entry.

---

8 www.tmdn.org/publicwebsite/#/
9 www.tmdn.org/tmdsview-web/#/dsview

> – Patentability examines prior art, assessing whether your invention is novel and inventive–regardless of whether those patents are active.
>
> Having freedom to operate does not guarantee an easy patenting process. Understanding both studies is key to mitigating risks and strengthening your IP strategy.

Patent landscaping

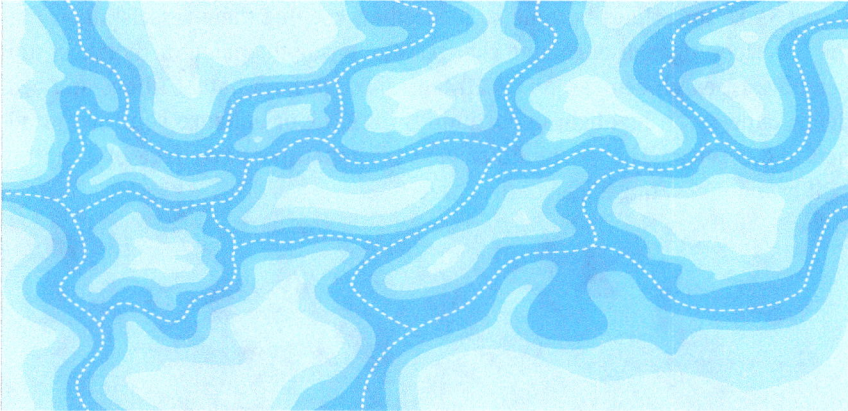

A patent landscape provides a comprehensive overview of patents within a specific field or technological domain, often visualised as a topographical chart. It enables innovators to gain deeper insight into the competitive environment and to identify potential opportunities and threats.

identify the rocks
Understanding the richness of the ocean begins with exploring the patent landscape in your sector or technology domain. While commissioning a full-scale landscape analysis can be expensive for start-ups, the insights gained can be transformative, revealing fertile areas for innovation, as well as densely patented regions where it is difficult to sail. Think of these as hidden rocks below the surface: Some are sharp (recent, active patents), others are softer (expired or non-harmful), but either way, they can impede your path to securing your own inventions.

anticipate the ripples

Looking only within your own field makes it harder to detect early signs of disruptions. Ripples in the water are more easily noticed if you scan adjacent markets for emerging trends and translate them into your own market. The rise of AI, for example, is causing ripples across countless sectors. Businesses that notice and adapt early stand a much better chance of steering clear of a future tsunami.

stay agile in an exponential era

With disruptive technologies emerging at an exponential pace, it is crucial to remain alert and, if possible, be the speedboat that generates the first ripples. Established SMEs sometimes become so focused on keeping their vessels afloat that they overlook signs of oncoming change. Monitoring the patent activities of universities, research centres, and R&D labs–through both patent filings and academic papers–can highlight opportunities to refine or enhance your own products and services. Those who do so gain a competitive advantage by adapting swiftly and innovating ahead of the curve.

Swarm

Operating as a speedboat in a swarm of vessels means you are collaborating with others. In such a scenario, you are most likely not developing your own product or service, but you are building a joined innovative journey. To secure your business in such a situation, it is important to prepare yourself.

Focusing too much on protection may be an indication that you are not open-minded enough to make the collaboration work. However, if you take the right steps to safeguard your interests while staying open to co-creation, collaboration can become a true adventure–one of growth, shared learning, and building products and services together.

Step 1: What precautions do you need to take prior to the collaboration?

Focus on your own speedboat:
– Define the purpose of the collaboration not only related to the groups effort, but especially to your own journey. How will it fit in your plans? Will it enrich your IP portfolio? Will your growth plans (and related IP strategy) not be hindered?
– What background knowledge is required for this collaboration? Are all necessary precautions in place (such as patent applications and know-how hidden descriptions)?

– Do you need to reveal trade secrets for the collaboration? Then have your NDA contracts prepared prior to in-depth discussions and avoid talking about these trade secrets in early orientation phases. Only release trade secrets if it is really necessary and have signed NDA-agreements first.

Focus on the other vessels in the collaboration:
– What is the business model of these vessels? Do they have an active IP strategy in place? What intellectual property rights do they have in place that might be relevant for the collaboration?
– Why would these vessels be interested in the collaboration? What could be their purpose? What would be their win? Are they in it just for the collaboration or is there a business interest to do so?
– What IP risks might be involved through the collaboration? Will they need to license some of their IP and at what terms?

Focus on the collaboration project:
– What would be the purpose of the project? And how will it match with your speedboat?
– What would potentially be the foreground knowledge and IP that will be created and in what sense would it be interfering with your company's IP?
– Could you detect synergy between the different vessels? What are the perfect matches and where do you see the clashes?
– Which expertise from your speedboat is relevant to the collaboration? Are you unique in this position or are there others (perhaps competition) involved?
– What would be possible business models for the collaboration?

A lot of questions to prepare, but crucial to any collaboration. They do not hinder the collaboration, instead they make the collaboration much more efficient.

And it is always better to be prepared. If you know your role, your strength and your challenges prior to the collaboration negotiations and you have gathered relevant insights on your collaboration partners, you will most likely succeed in finding a balanced collaboration agreement.

Step 2: Starting the collaborations

As a preparation, everybody needs to sign an NDA agreement, securing their own IP that is not publicly available.

Prior to the collaboration itself, you need to agree upon a collaboration agreement. This collaboration agreement needs to define what happens with the foreground IP created through the collaboration.

Too many collaborations start without any agreement. Companies can steal ideas or thoughts during such a phase without the obligation to safeguard the foreground IP created. Companies avoiding to sign NDA agreements or postponing the draft of a collaboration agreement, are definitely companies to investigate regarding their IP attitude.

Clearly define in the contract how the foreground knowledge will be handled.

Ask yourself the following questions:

– **Is the collaboration focused on research, with no direct commercial outcome?**
  In that case, are all parties allowed to use the resulting, and how does it relate to the background knowledge contributed by each party?
– **Is the collaboration business-oriented, with commercial goals?**
  If so, it is key to clarify:
  – Who is in charge of development?
  – Who will handle commercialisation?
  – How will you share IP?
  – Who will bear the costs, efforts, and potential risks?
  – And who stands to benefit, and in what way?

Tip

When drafting a collaboration agreement, make sure to clearly address the following key elements to avoid misunderstandings and ensure a solid foundation for your partnership.

- **Purpose**. Clearly define the objective and intent of the collaboration.
- **Definitions of key terms**. Provide precise definitions to avoid ambiguity throughout the agreement.
- **Scope and exclusions**. Specify the roles, responsibilities, and obligations of each party, as well as what is explicitly excluded from the agreement.
- **Duration and termination**. Outline the start and end dates, along with conditions for early termination.
- **Intellectual property**. Clarify ownership and usage rights of any IP created or shared during the collaboration.
- **Confidentiality and non-disclosure**. Include provisions to protect sensitive information exchanged between parties.
- **Financial arrangements and payment terms**. Detail the financial commitments, cost-sharing, invoicing, and payment schedules.
- **Performance and milestones**. Define expected deliverables, timelines, and how progress will be monitored.
- **Dispute resolution**. Establish a mechanism for resolving conflicts, preferably including mediation before resorting to legal proceedings.
- **Liability and indemnification**. Set out the responsibilities for damages or losses and any indemnity provisions.
- **Force majeure**. Address how unforeseeable events beyond either party's control will be handled.
- **Compliance with laws and regulations**. Ensure all activities within the agreement comply with applicable laws and regulatory requirements.
- **Governing law and jurisdiction**. Indicate which country's laws will govern the agreement and where any legal proceedings would take place.
- **Non-compete and exclusivity**. Specify any limitations on entering similar agreements with third parties.
- **Publicity and announcements**. Determine how and when information about the collaboration can be publicly shared.
- **Miscellaneous clauses**. Include any additional provisions such as amendments, severability, or assignment.

Step 3: at the end of the collaboration

Make sure you know what knowledge you are allowed to use based on the collaboration and if licenses on intellectual property (rights or know-how) are required to use that knowledge.

An open attitude towards innovation is always a better approach. Stepping too defensive into a collaboration, will not allow that project to achieve its full potential.

Beyond partnership: corporate venturing

While collaboration agreements focus on aligning mutual interests to achieve a shared objective, **corporate venturing** introduces a different dynamic. Unlike traditional partnerships, corporate venturing is driven by the long-term innovation or market positioning needs of the larger corporation. For young companies, it is essential to recognise that behind a corporate venturing proposal lies a broader business strategy–one that may not always be openly communicated. Understanding this (hidden) layer, is key to navigating the relationship effectively and securing your own strategic interests.

Corporates typically approach start-ups for two key reasons:

Technological and market interest
–   **Access to disruptive innovation**. Your start-up operates at the cutting edge and may accelerate their innovation roadmap.
–   **Skilled team**. Your crew brings expertise that can complement their R&D teams.
–   **Agility and risk reduction**. Start-ups can test new business models, markets, and technologies with lower risk for corporates.
–   **Market expansion**. If you operate in adjacent markets, collaboration can open new growth opportunities for both corporates and start-ups.

Strategic reasons
–   **Sustainability and social impact**. Aligning with an innovative start-up enhances corporate reputation.
–   **Financial potential**. Your business shows promising growth, making investments or collaboration an attractive proposition.

- **Competitive advantage**. Partnering with your start-up can help corporates gain an edge over industry rivals.

While such collaborations can provide resources and market access, they must be prepared and structured carefully to protect your business interests and IP.

Extra key points to consider in corporate venturing:
- Start-ups and corporates both bring **pre-existing IP** (e.g., proprietary technology or processes). Ensure your company retains control over its foundational IP.
- If the partnership leads to **co-developed innovations**, define who owns the rights. Corporates often push for exclusive rights, partly out of concern that young companies may lack the resources to properly claim and defend IPR. As a speedboat business, it is important to negotiate terms that still allow you some freedom to commercialise the technology independently, while addressing the corporate's need for legal certainty.
- IP may be **licensed** between parties, granting the corporate the right to use your technology. Ensure clear terms on scope, duration, sublicensing, and commercialisations.
- As sensitive IP will likely be shared, strict **NDAs** are essential. Prevent corporate partners from using your IP beyond the agreed scope, so that it does not end up in the hands of competitors or third parties.
- Corporates can provide **resources** to scale and commercialise your innovation. Define who has exclusive or shared commercialisation rights and profit-sharing models.
- Corporates may try to absorb or replicate your innovation. Implement contractual protections **limiting** their **use** of your IP.
- Ensure the collaboration **benefits** both parties without compromising your start-up's independence.

Corporate collaborations can offer funding, expertise, and market expansion, but without careful structuring, they can also put your IP and business autonomy at risk. A well-defined IP agreement ensures clarity on ownership, licensing, confidentiality, and commercialisation, helping both parties collaborate effectively while protecting your competitive advantage.

Wrapping up

This chapter has guided you through the complexities of securing your speedboat. Of course, these measures come at a cost. Sailing safely and avoiding costly litigation from third parties is one way to earn that investment back.

There is, however, another way to maximise the return on your IP investments: As you have seen in Chapter 3, IP is an asset–an intangible asset that should not be overlooked when seeking funding or preparing to sell your business.

Curious how your IP can strengthen your selling or funding journey? That is exactly what the next chapter will explore.

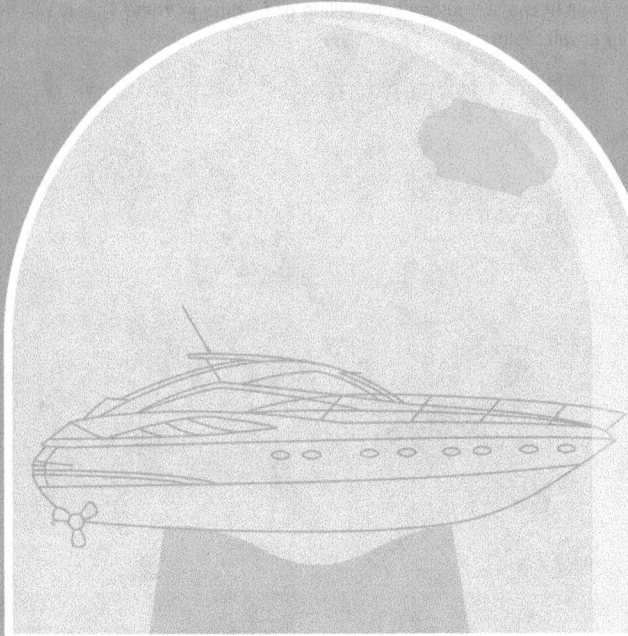

4

SELL OR FUND

https://doi.org/10.1515/9783111673547-004

4.0 Introduction

What to expect

How the measures outlined in Chapters 2 and 3 can deliver their full value by understanding their role in the investment, acquisition, and sales process.

As your speedboat business grows, you may seek additional funding or explore exit opportunities to avoid managing the growth entirely on your own. That is when the true ROI of your IP can be realised. That is when all your efforts–choosing the right IPR, building a cost-effective yet strategic IP approach, et cetera–become critical in securing the right valuation and negotiating the best deal.

Funding or sale processes typically occur while your company is still burning cash or just beginning to generate revenue. At this stage, your **intangible assets** play a vital role in demonstrating value. A well-structured IP portfolio can significantly impact investor confidence, funding potential, and acquisition price.

The more you understand:
- your IP assets and their market relevance
- how your IP choices impact business performance
- the strategic importance of your IP in negotiations

... the better positioned you are to secure funding or maximise your company's sale price.

At this stage, all the precautions and measures taken based on the parameters outlined in Chapters 2 and 3 come into play. There are three key elements to prepare when aiming for sale or seeking funding:
- **The strategic value of IP**. Both your IP management and your IP strategy should support current operations as well as future business growth.
- **Due diligence**. Your IP must be clearly structured and show an ROI, positioning it as a valuable asset during investor or buyer assessments.
- **Data room management**. Keeping your data room up to date should be part of your day-to-day business administration.

This chapter is a must-read for captains and strategic crew members. While external experts can assist you in this process, you cannot fully delegate it. As the captain, you need a strong grasp of the IP-related mechanics of funding and sale negotiations.

4.1 The strategic value of IP in the process of selling or funding

To maximise the value of your IP in a funding or sale process, you must understand the language of IP and its role in your business.

IP management

Simply outsourcing your IP management as a black box to third parties means you lose control over the process. While expert guidance is essential, you must personally grasp how IP contributes to your business and aligns with investor or buyer expectations. Inability to answer key IP-related questions during due diligence can lower your valuation.

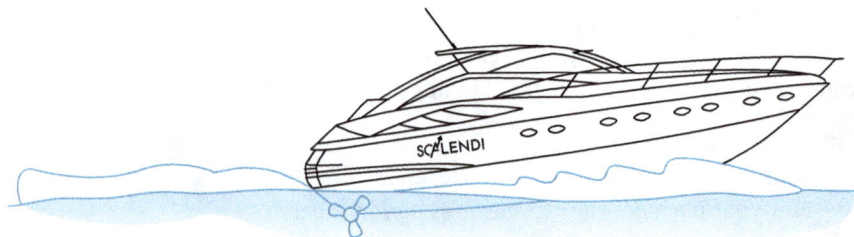

When selling or funding, the first check is whether your IP rights are properly secured, registered, and up to date. In Chapter 3, we connected IP rights to the key components of your speedboat:
– boat name > trademark
– hull > design/copyright
– engine > patent
– fuel > know-how
– fuel additives > trade secret

However, simply owning IP rights is not enough. Without a coherent IP strategy, they remain passive assets, offering little insight into how IP actively supports your business goals.

IP strategy

As a start-up or scale-up with limited resources, you have learned to make strategic IP choices (see Chapter 3, section Navigation system). A well-structured IP navigation system ensures you to make the right decisions at the right time, optimising investment in protection versus business needs and ambitions.

Having a strong IP strategy means that you understand:
–   IP rights and their relation to your business
–   how to strategically implement IPR, even with limited means
–   how to strategically align your IPR measures with your scalable growth
–   how this IP strategy plays a role in the valuation of your business

It also shows that, despite a limited budget, you made deliberate, strategic choices–focusing on securing your core business with IPR, while using alternative strategies for less critical elements. It is not a random selection, but a well-considered process.

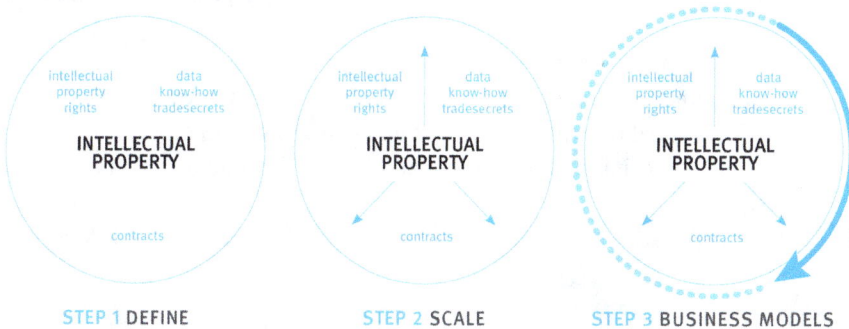

intellectual property rights	data know-how tradesecrets
INTELLECTUAL PROPERTY	
	contracts

STEP 1 DEFINE   STEP 2 SCALE   STEP 3 BUSINESS MODELS

Do not forget the three-step approach outlined in the Navigation system section of Chapter 3.

When you have such a strong strategy in place, you are ready for funding or sale, with your intangible assets playing a pivotal role in securing the best possible valuation. You are now able to explain through your IP pitch how your IP strategy plays an important role in the value and future growth of your company.

4.2 Due diligence

When investors or buyers consider funding or acquiring a company, they have specific motivations–whether financial, strategic, or societal. Their decision to invest is based on a careful assessment of opportunities and risks.

Where to start: finding the right investors or buyers

For early-stage funding, the first place to look is often within your personal network, such as family and friends. However, this typically provides only limited capital.

For scaling or selling a business, you will need to engage with professional investors or buyers, which requires strategic negotiations. Surrounding yourself with funding experts is essential–they understand the process, requirements, and potential pitfalls and will help you secure the best outcome.

Whether you are the one reaching out to investors or buyers or whether they approach you directly, never go into the process blindly. Engage experts and conduct your own research.
- Analyse their business strategy to understand their interest in your business.
- Assess alignment with your vision, mission, and future growth-plans.
- Identify potential risks in the partnership before committing.
- Use the tips and insights from Chapter 3 on the ecosystem to carry out this analysis.

Understanding the decision-making process of investors or buyers

Investors or buyers weigh potential returns against risks before making a decision. While you mainly see growth potential, they also analyse possible threats to their investment–some of which you may not even be aware of.

To evaluate this balance, investors or buyers conduct a so-called due diligence–a detailed risk assessment that examines:
- the viability of your business, aka the opportunities
- potential impact on their portfolio, aka the investments
- societal, financial, legal, and strategic considerations, aka the risks

Due diligence is typically carried out by a team of experts in finance, business strategy, and law.

Why due diligence preparation is essential

For start-ups and scale-ups, due diligence can feel overwhelming. If you are un-prepared, it can seriously weaken your position, leading to a lower valuation, which in turn may result in reduced funding or a lower sale price.

Preparing is key because you need to:
–   understand the due diligence process and its role in funding/selling negotiations
–   anticipate what investors or buyers will examine to strengthen your position

Avoiding all risks is impossible. Instead, acknowledge them transparently and ex-plain your strategy for managing them. Attempting to hide risks will only break or complicate the deal, resulting in less favourable contract terms.

Surprisingly, many small companies fail to prepare for due diligence, even though they would meticulously prepare for a certification process such as ISO 14000. By neglecting IP due diligence preparation, though, you miss valuable op-portunities and increase the risk of receiving a lower financial valuation.

The role of IP in due diligence

IP due diligence, in particular, is often undervalued, reduced to a basic count of reg-istered patents or trademarks. However, for start-ups and scale-ups, IP is a crucial intangible asset–and often the foundation of business growth and future scalability.

If your business is still burning cash rather than generating significant revenue, a strong IP strategy aligned with your business strategy can demonstrate:
–   how your IP creates competitive advantage
–   the role of your IP in securing long-term growth
–   the investment potential of your intangible assets

Effectively pitching your IP as an asset not only strengthens investor or buyer confidence but also signals business maturity. It shows that proactive measures have been taken to build scalable growth, making your company a far more at-tractive investment opportunity.

4.3 Data room management

A well-organised data room is essential for any due diligence process, whether for funding or selling. It serves as a centralised space–physical or virtual–where all key business information is stored and structured.

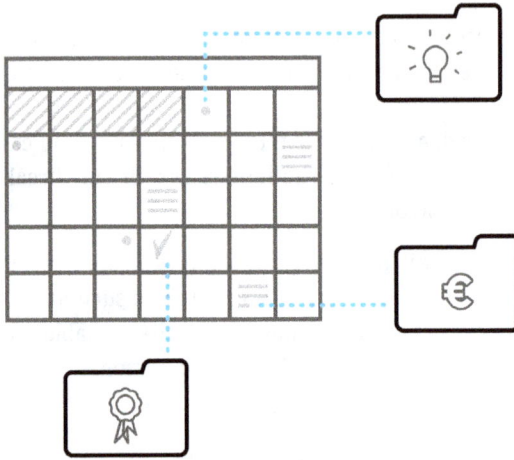

If you only start assembling your data room weeks before due diligence, you are too late and you risk missing critical opportunities. Instead, build and maintain it continuously, treating it as the lifeline of your business, reflecting the value of your business.

What to include in your IP data room

Content

Your IP data room should contain all measures summed up in Chapter 3, including:
- **contracts:** NDAs, employee agreements, supplier contracts
- **IPR:** patents, trademark, copyrights, trade secrets, including all administrative steps throughout the (post-)granting process

Store your IP data in line with your business and business strategy, and be as detailed as possible since each document plays a role in the risk assessment that comes with due diligence and may influence investor or buyer confidence.

Tools

New AI-driven legaltech tools are making data room building and management more efficient. This may come in handy for large corporations with an overload of data.

However, as a start-up, relying on AI too early may not be effective. Why?
- As the captain of your speedboat, building your data room manually first will give you a deeper understanding of your company's assets.
- You will learn to prioritise and structure critical information.
- You will identify common templates (e.g., NDAs) to streamline documentation.

Once your company grows and a structured routine for updating your data room is in place, AI can help automate organisation and improve searchability.

Tip

Set up a structured data room from the start:
1. Choose a secure, scalable platform for your data room (e.g., a virtual data room or cloud-based storage).
2. Create a clear, logical folder structure with categories such as company information, financials, legal documents, product details, HR, sales and marketing, and compliance.
3. Assign access rights based on roles and the sensitivity of the information.
4. Keep the data room up to date; regularly add new documents and maintain a clear structure.
5. Safeguard the data with encryption, regular backups, and strong authentication protocols.
6. Monitor the data room's performance and ensure it can scale with your company's growth.

By setting up a structured and secure data room from the outset, you will not only protect your company's sensitive information but also make it far easier to share with investors, partners, or potential buyers when the time comes.

Know-how and trade secrets

Though often overlooked when building a data room, your know-how and trade secrets are crucial for business continuity and must be documented carefully. This is particularly important during a merger round, as there is no guarantee that key team members (particularly freelancers) will remain once you sell your company.
- **Software**: Explain the reasoning behind coding. Use flow charts to illustrate the relationship between different modules.

- **Data**: Provide a tree structure to explain data architecture and relationships.
- **Formulas and recipes**: Detail each ingredient's role and impact.
- **Design**: Show how customer insights are translated into unique features.
- **Research**: Keep lab books documenting experiments securely stored–never leave them unattended.

Without proper documentation, investors or buyers may demand that you and your key crew members stay on board for years–a major consideration in any merger or acquisition. It increases the risk for an investor and will definitely result in a lower valuation.

Since you cannot reveal this information upfront–as long as the merger has not been guaranteed, revealing this information is too risky–you need to take extra measures for example through NDA contracts.

A well-prepared data room demonstrates professionalism, reduces risks, and adds value to your business. By ensuring structured documentation and proactive knowledge management, you strengthen your company's investment appeal and long-term security.

Wrapping up

By now, you have seen how to build and secure your speedboat–and specifically in Chapter 4, you have learned that if you follow the steps outlined in Chapters 2 and 3, your IP investments can become powerful leverage when negotiating funding or preparing to sell your company. In short, you now understand that IP is a valuable asset, and a key driver of growth.

Still, even with that understanding, it might be challenging to apply these principles to your day-to-day business. That is exactly what Chapter 5 is here for. Through the *Light Buddy* case, you will see how to put everything from this book into practice, and you will get a final suggestion on how to chart your own course forward.

Chapter 5
From insight to action

https://doi.org/10.1515/9783111673547-005

5.0 Introduction

What to expect

A practical and concrete start-up story that walks you through the entire process, showing how you can apply the insights from this book to your own journey.

Understanding IP and IPR is a lot to take in–but the key is not just knowing that they exist, but recognising how they can serve as valuable assets to your company.

This means that, as your business evolves, so should your IP strategy. As a start-up and scale-up, you are still defining and refining your business model, exploring different markets and applications, and developing your entrepreneurial skills. Unlike larger companies with well-established products or services, your offerings are likely still evolving–requiring improvements, design changes, or even major pivots. This evolution directly impacts your IP choices.

With tight budgets, investing in IPR–especially patents–too early can be risky. If your invention evolves beyond its original scope, your patent may no longer align with your final product or service, making the investment ineffective.

As a young company, you need to think ahead:
- How will your core technology and business model evolve?
- What elements are scalable and future-proof?
- How can you structure IP choices that support growth for at least five years?

By structuring your IP roadmap strategically, you can safeguard your innovations while staying agile and adaptable in an ever-changing market.

5.1 How Light Buddy BV proceeded

To bring IP strategy and management to life, this chapter introduces a fictional business case: the Light Buddy start-up. Designed to illustrate how theory can be put into practice, the Light Buddy case walks you through the key steps of securing and strengthening a start-up through IP decisions. Though entirely imaginary, the scenario reflects common challenges and opportunities faced by early-stage ventures–offering clear, relatable insights into what IP can mean for your business.

The birth of an IDEA

Peter, a PhD expert in drone technology and an avid trail runner, often found himself running in low-light conditions. Frustrated by poor visibility, he imagined a light that could autonomously follow and illuminate his path–freeing him from the limitations of wearable devices.

As Peter explored the idea further through mentoring and brainstorming sessions, the concept evolved. No longer just a runner's gadget, the innovation became a versatile autonomous lighting system, able to direct light where needed in a hands-free manner. The initial use case in outdoor sports quickly expanded to include security and industrial maintenance applications.

With his deep technological expertise and growing confidence in the business potential, Peter decided to launch a start-up: Light Buddy BV.

Building their speedboat business

People

Although technically brilliant, Peter lacked business experience. To complement his skills, he teamed up with Sofie, a seasoned business developer with expertise in marketing, operations, and people management. Together, they formed a strong, balanced founding team.

After drafting a business plan, they engaged specialised freelancers in drone technology, miniaturisation, and lighting to build a Minimum Viable Product (MVP). Once the early prototypes proved successful, they brought in full-time staff to support testing, production, and day-to-day operations.

To accelerate growth, they partnered with university research groups for product expertise and joined start-up incubators for strategic guidance and mentorship on achieving product-market fit.

Construction

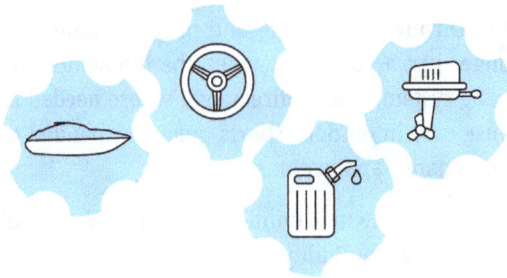

Light Buddy BV's mission is to bring autonomous lighting wherever it's needed, with their first product aimed at outdoor sports and leisure. Peter and Sophie conducted in-depth market research and developed detailed user personas to ensure a strong product-market fit. Their service-design-driven approach shaped a product that wasn't just functional, but desirable–a smart, wearable-free lighting companion.

While initially targeting the sports market, Peter and Sofie built a technology platform that was flexible and scalable. Their MVP focused on essential features, with modular components that allowed for quick adaptation across markets.

Their unfair advantage lay in Peter's drone expertise, which helped them overcome early technical barriers and speed up development. Funding came from a mix of grants, loans, and early-stage investors, while strategic networking opened doors to market entry. Brainstorming sessions and mentoring revealed broader commercial potential beyond outdoor sports, encouraging a flexible mindset and ongoing market exploration.

Ecosystem

To keep pace with fast-evolving technologies, they collaborated with research partners to monitor advancements in miniaturisation, drone control, and lighting. They studied competitors both locally and internationally. While there were no direct European competitors, they identified FoxFury in Asia as a partial alternative, albeit without full autonomy.

Rather than trying to do everything in-house, they partnered with a lighting company, allowing them to focus on their core: drone navigation and miniaturisation. Their adaptable technology quickly attracted interest from sectors like security and maintenance, paving the way for future licensing opportunities.

Securing their speedboat business

Construction

To protect their innovation, Peter and Sofie took a strategic approach to intellectual property. They invested in design protection for the outdoor version of their product, which combines utility with a stylish, sports-friendly aesthetic. This ensured that the product would not only function well, but also appeal to consumers as a lifestyle gadget.

Their overall business strategy–how they navigated market selection, pricing, and timing–was considered proprietary knowledge and kept confidential. These insights, refined through experience and mentoring, became part of the company's competitive edge.

At the core of their IP portfolio was a single, scalable patent that covered the autonomous, miniaturised drone-light system. Instead of filing sector-specific patents, they included use cases across outdoor sports, security, and maintenance in one well-crafted application. This choice reduced costs while keeping the door open for future expansion.

Given budget constraints, they prioritised protecting the drone's manoeuvrability and miniaturisation–technologies with high cross-sector value. Lighting innovations were intentionally left unpatented, allowing university partners to publish findings and create prior art, effectively blocking others from patenting similar ideas.

This smart, selective IP approach bolstered their credibility and supported future funding discussions.

People

To formalise their collaboration, Peter and Sofie drafted a founders' agreement covering ownership, growth terms, and exit strategies–recognising Peter's original idea and technical expertise as key intangible contributions.

Freelancers and employees signed contracts outlining IP rights, confidentiality, and non-compete clauses. All contributions made during their engagement belonged to Light Buddy BV, though inventors were properly credited. A structured process ensured regular reviews of sensitive information, including how trade secrets were protected from external exposure.

Partner organisations and research centres signed collaboration agreements with clearly defined terms for IP ownership and confidentiality. External publications required prior internal approval, and all IP developed remained the property of Light Buddy BV.

Ecosystem

Light Buddy BV kept a close watch on the IP landscape. They set up alerts for new patents, monitored competitors' filings, and regularly performed freedom-to-operate analyses. While no immediate legal risks were found, they understood that new patents may only become visible after 18 months, warranting continued vigilance.

They also mapped areas of opportunity for new patent applications, targeting technological gaps and strengthening their innovation portfolio.

With a strong, flexible IP position, they began negotiating licensing opportunities in security and maintenance markets–offering exclusive access or joint development in return for market entry and financial leverage.

Attracting investment

As the company grew, so did its financial needs. Aware of the runway limits, Peter and Sofie prepared a compelling pitch–not just focused on financial forecasts, but also highlighting their robust IP strategy and market readiness.

Their selective patenting approach was a key asset. Rather than blanket protection, they made strategic choices: patent what added cross-market value, publish what could block competitors, and keep trade secrets that could not easily be reverse-engineered. This nuanced approach impressed investors who valued both innovation and cost-efficiency.

Investor-readiness and due diligence

Understanding that due diligence could make or break a deal, they prepared thoroughly. Their documentation included financials, a clear business plan, and a roadmap explaining how IP reinforced their competitive position and scalability.

They also created an IP pitch deck, clearly demonstrating how their protection strategy aligned with business growth and investor interests.

Data and knowledge management

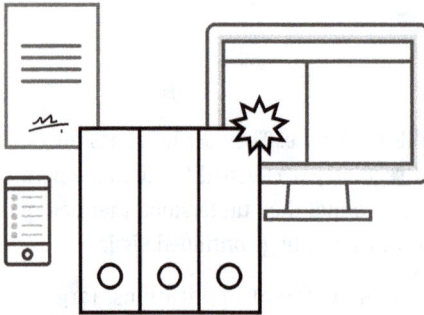

From the start, Light Buddy BV had built a structured data room, organising contracts, IP filings, and critical know-how. This facilitated internal decision-making, ensured knowledge continuity, and built investor confidence.

Looking ahead, they explored automation tools to improve IP tracking and legal documentation–future-proofing their internal processes and minimising risk.

The outcome for light buddy NV

With a strong technological foundation, a well-defined business strategy, and a clear roadmap for growth, Light Buddy BV is set to revolutionise autonomous lighting. By strategically leveraging their expertise, partnerships, and IP assets, they are now well-positioned to secure funding and expand into multiple markets, ensuring their place at the forefront of innovation.

5.2 How to proceed yourself

Enough about Peter and his company Light Buddy BV, now it is your turn.

As you grow your business, what are the key steps to securing it, and how will you find the answers within this book?

When taking your business public, scaling, or seeking investment, you must ensure that your speedboat business is built on a solid, secure foundation. This process involves three essential steps.

Step 1: speedboat check-up

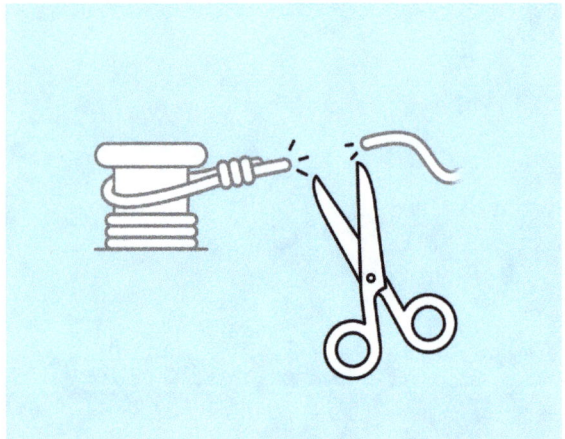

Before you reveal your business to the world, you need to perform a thorough check-up to ensure your speedboat is ready to sail:

Do you have FTO?

Before launching, verify that your business does not infringe on existing IP rights. (Double) check trademarks, designs, and especially patents to avoid costly litigation or business disruptions. The last thing you want is to be forced to stop operations just as you begin.

Thus, in this stage, the analysis of your ecosystem is crucial.

What is your own IP strategy?

Understanding the (potential) IP within your speedboat business and developing a clear strategy to navigate your speedboat is key. On top of that, your speedboat's construction will define the IP protection measures you need.

Timing is everything

Apply for the necessary IP rights **before** going public. If you exhibit your innovation at a trade fair, launch online, or even only discuss it openly, you may lose the opportunity to secure protection. Use this book as a checklist to ensure you have covered all critical steps in securing your business.

Step 2: speedboat maintenance

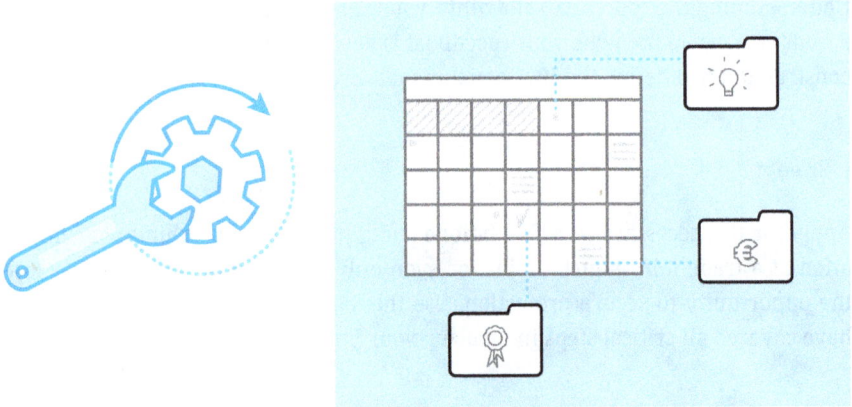

Once your speedboat is in motion, maintaining the balance between innovation, entrepreneurship, and IP strategy is critical.

Monitor your ecosystem

Just like you, your competitors and market landscape will continue to evolve. Stay alert to new technologies that could either pose a risk or create an opportunity to boost your business. Regularly monitor IPR of your competitors and industry trends to stay ahead.

Maintain and adapt your IP strategy

As your business grows, so should your IP strategy evolve.

Conduct monthly check-ups on:
- your innovation plans and new developments
- your potential rebranding and new designs
- ongoing IP registrations and whether they still align with your business

This helps ensure that IP remains a priority and does not get buried under day-to-day operations.

Verify whether your IP strategy and your speedboat's navigation system are still aligned.

The more you scale, the more exposure you will have. Without continuous updates, your IP security weakens.

Follow up on your IP

Once you have applied for patents, trademarks, et cetera, remember that securing IP is not a one-time event. You must continuously respond to legal challenges and comply with regulations.

Keep track of your know-how, and regularly identify which information is crucial and should be treated as confidential or even as a trade secret. Put a knowledge management system in place.

Ensure you have reliable IP strategists–acting as translator-interpreters–who keep you informed and guide you towards measures that support your business growth.

Strengthen your team and IP assets

As your speedboat business grows, so does the importance of securing your team and intellectual assets. Before hiring new employees or external support, ensure that you have:
– IP-focused contracts and measures covering know-how, trade secrets, and confidentiality
– a structured and continuously updated data room containing all critical IP and legal documents
– a systematic approach to tracking and managing these assets, such as setting up regular IP-focused meetings and integrating IP aspects in development discussions and processes

Step 3: speedboat clean-up

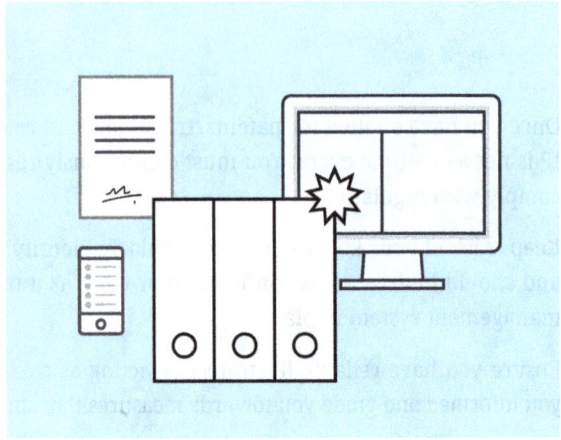

If you are preparing for funding, selling, or major partnerships, your business needs to be in perfect shape. Investors or potential buyers will scrutinise every detail–a process known as due diligence.

Is your data room ready?

When external experts review your company, will they find a readable, well-organised data room?

Ensure:
- your IP rights are well-documented, with clear timelines and status updates
- software documentation includes flow charts, database trees, et cetera visualising the set-up
- mechanical design drawings, user manuals, and electrical schematics are up-to-date, clearly labelled, and include explanatory notes where needed
- trade secrets are defined, secured, and contribute to your growth strategy
- You have a knowledge management system in place
- contracts are easily accessible, with summaries of key elements such as purpose, parties, and duration

Strengthen your IP assets for negotiations

Before engaging themselves, investors want to estimate risks, opportunities, and ROI. This means a fleet of (financial, legal, technological) experts will control all ins and outs of your company, not just financial aspects or patents, but also your IP strategy as a whole.

So be prepared to pitch your IP strategy and how it supports your growth:
- Explain your assets.
- Explain how they give you a competitive advantage.
- Explain how they can boost your growth.
- Explain what IP measures are in place.
- Explain the internal procedures to support and maintain your assets.

> **Wrapping up**
>
> A high-performance IP management and strategy does not just provide legal protection–it is a business asset. Whether preparing to go public, maintaining growth, or seeking invest-ment, ensuring your speedboat is–and remains–secure, makes for smoother sailing and a stronger, more valuable company.
>
> By following these three steps, you ensure your IP works for you, rather than becoming a liability–helping you grow with confidence while safeguarding your competitive advantage.
>
> I sincerely hope you have discovered how to identify and build scalable intellectual property for your speedboat business and that you now recognise IP as a valuable asset for sustain-able, scalable growth.
>
> Wishing you the very best of luck in all your future endeavours!

Acknowledgments

I would like to express my heartfelt gratitude to:

My late father, who sparked my passion for intellectual property by sharing his excitement whenever one of his patents was granted during his time as an engineer.

My former employers, peers in the IP field, influential voices in the industry, and professional networks such as VLAIO, BEPIUG and LES Benelux, all of whom gave me the opportunity to learn about IP and IP management. I am also thankful for the many insightful webinars organised by the High Growth Technology Forum, the EPO, and LESI.

Most of all, I want to thank my clients during my time as an IP and innovation consultant. They openly shared their challenges around IP and innovation, trusted me to guide them through their first steps in applying for patents, and helped me understand the barriers they faced with the language of IP. Through them, I learned to become an interpreter and translator in IP matters–an experience that ultimately led to this book.

From the first idea to write a book to holding the final publication in my hands, it has been a true journey of personal growth and perseverance.

A special thanks goes to Emilie, my business development assistant, who helped turn the dream of writing this book into a reality.

https://doi.org/10.1515/9783111673547-006

About the author

Throughout her career, An Cosaert has worked at the intersection of innovation, entrepreneurship, and intellectual property. Fascinated by technology and the way new ideas can transform industries, she first set out to pursue a degree in industrial engineering electromechanics. Thus equipped with a strong analytical mindset and a broad technical foundation, she started her professional journey at KU Leuven, where she conducted research on textile composites.

Switching the academic world for R&D at various international corporates, she gained hands-on experience in material applications and learned how technology translates into real-world industrial solutions. This environment allowed her to refine her ability to translate complex technical concepts into clear and accessible knowledge.

In 2007, she took a pivotal step in her career by becoming an innovation consultant and expert, first at the West Flanders Innovation Centre and later on at Antwerp Management School. Here, she discovered her passion for guiding start-ups, scale-ups and SMEs through their innovation processes. She gained deep insights into the strategic importance of IP and developed methods to make IP more accessible and actionable for entrepreneurs (in the making), thus bridging the gap between innovative ideas and scalable business models.

Since 2018, she is teaching Intellectual Property Strategy at Antwerp Management School (Master programme Sustainable Innovation & Entrepreneurship).

In 2019, she started her own consultancy agency Inquirendi (Latin for "on a discovery") bringing together innovation, entrepreneurship, and IP. Since then, she has been helping companies future-proof their innovation and IP strategies and support them in building scalable, sustainable, technology-driven businesses.

Recently, she expanded her ventures with Scalendi (Latin for "scaling"), an agency that focuses on developing IP strategies that support the scaling or growth of companies, through business model alignment and IP due diligence preparation.

It is not only her mission, but also her passion to make intellectual property both achievable and strategically valuable for businesses navigating an ever-evolving world.

https://doi.org/10.1515/9783111673547-007

Glossary

Symbols and abbreviations

Symbols

- ©: copyright; added by the creator of the work, preferably with an indication of time.
- ®: a registered trademark and can only be used by the people or the organisation that has applied for the trademark and has received approval by the Trademark office.
- ™: a trademark that is not registered yet; may be under application, but approval has not yet been granted.
- CC: Creative Commons.

Abbreviations

Offices
- EUIPO: European Union Intellectual Property Office
- EPO: European Patent Office
- BOIP: Benelux Office for Intellectual Property
- WIPO: World Intellectual Property Organization
- USPTO: United States Patent and Trademark Office
- CNIPA: China National Intellectual Property Administration
- EAPO: Eurasian Patent Office
- INTA: International Trademark Association

Patent-related
- FTO: Freedom To Operate
- PCT: Patent Cooperation Treaty
- IPC: International Patent Classification (worldwide used)
- CPC: Cooperative Patent Classification (extension of IPC and managed by both EPO and USPTO)
- FRAND: Fair, Reasonable and Non-discriminatory
- SEP: Standard Essential Patent

https://doi.org/10.1515/9783111673547-008

Patent number coding in Europe

E.g., EP0853901A3

Prefix

- EP: European Patent
- BE: Belgian Patent
- XX: Country code

IP glossary

Cease and desist notice: denoting a legally enforceable order from a court or government agency directing someone to stop engaging in a particular activity.

Contract clauses: specific sections within a contract that define certain rights, responsibilities and obligations.

Copyright: provides creators of original works, such as literature, music, films, and software, with exclusive rights to use and distribute their work.

Counterfeit: a fraudulent imitation of something else.

Descriptive seizure regarding counterfeiting: a procedure that allows the holder of an intellectual property right such as patents or designs to obtain evidence from the premises of an alleged infringer without any warning.

Divisional patent: a patent application that is filed later than the priority patent application while maintaining the original patent filing date and claiming the same priority date. Divisional patents use the information from the priority document but change or slightly apply the focus of the patent claims compared to the original.

Espacenet: free access patent database with worldwide coverage and search features.

Freedom To Operate (FTO): freedom to use, produce or sell a product or service without the possibility of infringements since no intellectual property rights are hindering your plans.

I-depot: a registration system by the Benelux Trademark Office that allows individuals and businesses to record ideas, concepts or creations with a trusted third party, serving as evidence of authorship and date of creation.

Industrial design: covers the visual appearance of a product, including its shape, configuration, patterns, or ornamentation, rather than its functional aspects.

Infringement: the violation or breach of a law, rule, or right. In the context of intellectual property (IP), it specifically means the unauthorised use, reproduction, or distribution of something protected by IP laws, such as patents, copyrights, trademarks, or trade secrets.

Inventive step: when a person skilled in the art, finds the description of a patent non obvious, conclusion can be made that the invention involves an inventive step.

Inventorship: the creator of an invention. Not to be confused with ownership that is related to the person or organisation that has the right to own that invention. In terms of patents, the owner is the applicant and the inventor is recognised as inventor without ownership.

IP asset: any material related to the intellectual property of an organisation that provides value for a business. Not just focused on intellectual property rights but on know-how and trade secrets as well.

IP culture: a company's internal awareness and approach to intellectual property, ensuring that employees understand the value of IP, follow best practices and contribute to securing innovations.

IP enforcement: the act of taking legal action when IP rights such as trademarks, copyrights, industrial designs, patents have been infringed.

IP monopoly: through the use of an intellectual property right, in most cases patents, the organisation owns a legal monopoly on a successful invention. The monopoly indicates that the owner of that IP right is the single seller or producer and there are no close substitutes.

IP policy: a structured plan that outlines how a business manages intellectual property, including its creation, ownership and use.

IP portfolio: the collection of all intellectual property assets owned or controlled by a company, including patents, trademarks, copyrights and trade secrets, strategically managed to support business growth.

IP registrations: intellectual property rights that are allocated to a registration procedure.

IP warranty: the disclosure or reassurance by a seller or service provider that, to its knowledge, the goods or services do not infringe on any patent, trademark, or other intellectual property right of a third party.

Knowledge background: the amount of information or know-how someone or an organisation has on a particular topic at a given time. In terms of collaboration it is important to define that background knowledge.

Knowledge foreground: all information (including data and/or results) that is generated through a project by a person or organisation. In terms of collaboration it is important to define what is considered to be foreground knowledge and what IP measures will be taken amongst the parties to secure this knowledge.

Knowledge management: the process of capturing, distributing and using knowledge. With respect to intellectual property, it also defines knowledge as value for an organisation and integrates the focus on IP strategy within knowledge management.

Lab book: a systematically maintained notebook where experiments, ideas and developments are recorded, providing a documented timeline of innovation.

License agreement: a formal agreement giving someone permission to use or do something not only related to intellectual property rights but know-how as well.

Licensing: granting permission to an organisation or licensee to use, produce or sell a product or service that is secured through intellectual property rights which you own as a licensor. Without the license, it would be considered as an infringement.

Litigation: refers to the process of taking legal action or resolving a dispute in court. It is the formal process of suing or defending a lawsuit in a legal context.

Non compete: a clause in a contract stating that parties or persons are not allowed to compete.

Non Disclosure Agreement (NDA): an agreement as a strategy of keeping information confidential to prevent others from copying or claiming it, commonly applied to trade secrets and innovative business models.

Non obvious: a person skilled in the art recognises that the invention was not easily discoverable or obvious.

Novelty: indication that the boundaries of a patent claim are new to the prior art.

Patent: grants exclusive rights to an invention, preventing others from making, using, or selling it without permission for a limited period.

Patent claims: define the boundaries of an invention and define the scope of a patent. They define the rules of what a patent covers or does not cover.

Patent examination: performed by an official patent examiner. The process of reading and understanding the invention within a patent application in order to determine whether it meets the patent criteria and the claims are clear in defining their boundaries. Can only start 18 months after filing date in order to have access to all prior art documents.

Patent Cooperation Treaty (PCT): a process that allows to apply for patent protection simultaneously in each of a large number of countries by filing an international patent application. (source: WIPO)

Prior use: the proof through date stamp, written documents or public exposure that a product or service was used before a priority date of an intellectual property right owned by a third party.

Skilled in the art: a person who is able to comprehend all technical matters regarding the state of the art in the field to which an invention belongs.

State of the art: the most recent stage in the development of a product, including newest technologies, ideas and features.

Third parties: external individuals, organisations or entities that interact with a company without being directly employed or integrated into its structure, such as suppliers, consultants or business partners.

Time stamp: a marker indicating that an idea, design, or concept is considered intellectual property, often established through documentation, contracts, or digital certification.

Trade secret: protects confidential business information, such as formulas, processes, or strategies, which provide a competitive advantage if kept undisclosed.

Trademark: protects distinctive signs such as logos, brand names, or slogans that identify and distinguish goods or services from competitors.

Glossary

Artificial Intelligence: the field of science related to building computers and machines that can reason, learn, and act in such a way that normally requires human intelligence or that involves data whose scale exceeds what humans can analyse.

Benchmarking: the process of comparing your product, services and processes against those of competitive organisations.

Business model: a plan to identify several business aspects such as customers, finance, and revenue in order to make profit.

Business model thinking: a strategic approach that helps organisations create, deliver and capture value. It is the exercise of varying business models to a certain product or service, in order to detect the plans that lead to profit.

Customer centricity: the practice of prioritising focus on the customer throughout all actions and attitude by an organisation.

Design Of Experiments (DOE): applied statistics that deal with planning, conducting, analysing and interpreting controlled tests. With the use of DOE, a research can be done with less experiments and still obtain statistical relevant results.

Design thinking: a non-linear, visually supported, iterative process that organisations use to understand users, challenge assumptions, redefine problems and create innovative solutions.

Emerging technology: a new technology that is ready to become applicable in industry and has passed fundamental research status. These technologies are defined by radical novelty, fast growth, coherence, prominent impact, uncertainty and ambiguity.

Freelancer: independent professional who provides services on a contract basis without being employed by a single company, often working on short-term or project-based assignments.

Incubator: programmes and hubs built to help start-ups with all aspects of starting their business from finding a workplace to funding.

Lean Startup Canvas: a one-page business plan that assists in analysing your product or business model through questioning and testing assumptions in order to define if your assumptions are viable. The methodology was created by Ash Maurya.

Merger & Acquisition (M&A): refers to possibilities for businesses to consolidate or combine their assets. When two separate entities combine their assets to form a new, joined entity, we call this a merger. An acquisition is when an organisation is completely taken over by an other entity.

Minimum Viable Product (MVP): a version of a product that includes only the essential features needed to test its market fit. It allows you to quickly validate whether your offering resonates with your target audience and effectively addresses their needs and desires.

Return On Investments (ROI): the measure used to evaluate the efficiency of an investment. The ROI on a development project can be calculated by defining the time needed to gain revenue equal to the development investment.

Software as a Service (SaaS): a cloud-based software delivery model where applications are hosted by a provider and accessed by users via the internet, typically on a subscription basis.

Scenario planning: a strategic planning process based on varying scenarios to gather assumptions on the future and how this will interfere with your business.

Service design: visual methodology to improve services based on tools that plan or arrange people, infrastructure, communication, et cetera.

Small or Medium-sized Enterprise (SME): small and medium-sized companies, defined by criteria such as number of employees, annual turnover, and/or balance sheet total. In the EU, a small enterprise typically has fewer than 50 employees and an annual turnover or balance sheet total of €10 million or less, whereas a medium-sized enterprise has fewer than 250 employees and an annual turnover of €50 million or less.

Societal challenges: issues related to health, demographics, wellbeing, food, sustainability, et cetera that impact the global society and require efforts by public, private and non-profit actors in order to be successfully resolved or at least improved.

Subcontractor: companies or individuals hired by a primary contractor to perform specific tasks or services within a larger project, often under defined terms and conditions

Sustainable Developments Goals (SDGs): adopted by the United Nations in 2015 as a call to action to end poverty, protect the planet and ensure that by 2030 all people enjoy peace and prosperity. The goals recognise that action in one area will affect outcomes in others, meaning that development needs to balance social, economic and environmental sustainability.

SWOT analysis: a study to identify Strengths vs Weaknesses and Opportunities vs Threats.

Sources and inspiring reads

[1] Angrave, J. (2020). *The Journey Mapping Playbook: A Practical Guide to Preparing, Facilitating and Unlocking the Value of Customer Journey Mapping*. Walter de Gruyter GmbH & Co KG.

[2] Bader, M. A., & Süzeroğlu-Melchiors, S. (2023). *Intellectual property management for start-ups: Enhancing Value and Leveraging the Potential*. Springer.

[3] Bakker, C. (2019). *Products that last: Product Design for Circular Business Models*. BIS Publishers.

[4] Boicova-Wynants, M. (2024) *Intellectual Property*, independently published.

[5] Cali R. & al., (2022). *50+ IP Hacks*, independently published.

[6] Cassady, B. (2021). *Cycles: The simplest, proven method to innovate faster while reducing risks*. Die Keure Publishing.

[7] Chan Kim, W. & Mauborgne, R. (2005). *Blue Ocean Strategy*, Harvard Business Review Press.

[8] Christensen, C. (2013). *The innovator's dilemma: When New Technologies Cause Great Firms to Fail*. Harvard Business Review Press.

[9] Collins, J. (2010). *Good to Great*, Business Contact.

[10] De Clercq, I. (2024). *Shaping Company Culture*. Pelckmans.

[11] Dessers, D. (2020). *Innovate. collaborate. grow!: Strategies and Best Practices for Corporate Partnering*. Die Keure Publishing.

[12] Dutt, R. (2021). *Radical product thinking: The New Mindset for Innovating Smarter*. Berrett-Koehler Publishers.

[13] Gray, I. & Bessant, J. (2024) *The scaling value Playbook*, Walter de Gruyter GmbH & Co KG.

[14] Haffmans, S., Van Gelder, M., Van Hinte, E., & Zijlstra, Y. (2018). *Products that flow: Circular Business Models and Design Strategies for Fast Moving Consumer Goods*. Bis Publishers.

[15] Hillner, M. (2021). *Intellectual property, design innovation, and entrepreneurship*. Springer Nature.

[16] Ismail S., Malone M.S., Van Geest, Y. & Diamandis, P. H. (2014). *Exponential Organizations*. Diversion Books.

[17] Jeyakodi, D., & Ros, M. (2019). *The innovation Matrix: Three Moves to Design a Winning Strategy for Innovation and Intellectual Property*. Bis Publishers.

[18] Jolly, A. (2013) *The Innovation Handbook 3rd edition*. Kogan Page Limited.

[19] Jolly, A. (2021). *Winning with IP: Managing High-growth Intellectual Property*. Novaro Publishing.

[20] Jones, P., & Van Ael, K. (2022). *Design journeys through complex systems: Practice Tools for Systemic Design*.

[21] Kokshagina, O., & Alexander, A. (2020). *The Radical Innovation Playbook: A Practical Guide for Harnessing New, Novel or Game-Changing Breakthroughs*. Walter de Gruyter GmbH & Co KG.

[22] Lanting M. (2019). *Olietankers en speedboten*. Business Contact.

[23] List, J. A. (2022). *The voltage effect: How to Make Good Ideas Great and Great Ideas Scale*. Currency.

[24] Marçal, K. (2021). *Mother of Invention: How good ideas get ignored in a world built for men*. HarperCollins UK.

[25] Masters, B., & Thiel, P. (2014). *Zero to one: Notes on Start Ups, or How to Build the Future*. Random House.

[26] Mattes, F. (2021). *Lean scaleup*. Lean Scaleup Ug.

[27] Maurya, A. (2018) Startup Lean. Nubiz.

[28] Moenaert, R. & Robben, H. (2022). *The Customer Leader*. S2 Uitgevers.

[29] Ohr, R., & Mattes, F. (2018). *Scaling-up corporate startups: Turn Innovation Concepts Into Business Impact*.

https://doi.org/10.1515/9783111673547-009

[30]   Ostyn, K. & Scherpereel, C. (2019). *Het oneerlijk voordeel.*

[31]   Phaal, R., Farrukh, C. J. P., & Probert, D. (2010). *Roadmapping for strategy and innovation: Aligning Technology and Markets in a Dynamic World.*

[32]   Pike, C. G., (2001). *Virtual Monopoly,* Nicholas Brealey Publishing.

[33]   Poltorak A.I. & Lerner P.J., (2004) *Essentials of Licensing Intellectual Property,* John Wiley& Sons.

[34]   Ries, E. (2017) *The Lean Startup,* Random House LCC US.

[35]   Rognstad, O. (2018). *Property aspects of intellectual property.*

[36]   Schweiger, M. (2021). *The 4x4 Innovation Strategy (Version 1.1).* Lulu Press, Inc.

[37]   Smith, K. R. (2021), *Start-up to Scale-up,* Novaro Publishing.

[38]   Undheim T. A. (2021). *Future Tech.* Kogan Page Limited.

[39]   Van Wulfen, G. (2022). *Online innovation: Tools, Techniques, Methods and Rules to Innovate Online.* Bis Publishers.

[40]   Verhoeve P. & Deschrijver, H. (2021). *Win-winnovation.* Bibliodroom.

[41]   Viki, T. (2020). *Pirates In The Navy: How Innovators Lead Transformation.* Unbound Publishing.

[42]   Viki, T., Toma, D., & Gons, E. (2019). *The corporate startup: How Established Companies Can Develop Successful Innovation Ecosystems.* Boom Uitgevers.

[43]   Wright, D. M., & Meadows, D. H. (2008). *Thinking in systems.* https://cds.cern.ch/record/1608083.

[44]   Yates, L. K. (2022). *The unicorn within: How Companies Can Create Game-Changing Ventures at Startup Speed.* Harvard Business Press.

Index

https://doi.org/10.1515/9783111673547-010

www.ingramcontent.com/pod-product-compliance
Lightning Source LLC
Chambersburg PA
CBHW061256220326
41599CB00028B/5669